Concord:

Its Poets
&
Its Places

Concord:

Its Poets
&
Its Places

Photographs by Rodger P. Nordblom and Mary W. Nordblom

and selected writings of
Louisa May Alcott
Ralph Waldo Emerson
Henry David Thoreau
Nathaniel Hawthorne

Edited by Nancy Richardot Tenney

Odin Press
Concord, Massachusetts

Published by
Odin Press, Concord, Massachusetts

Printed in the United States of America
ISBN: 0-9652175-0-7

Excerpts from the published writings of
Ralph Waldo Emerson by permission of the
Ralph Waldo Emerson Memorial Association.

Excerpts from the published writings of
Louisa May Alcott by permission of the
literary heirs of Louisa May Alcott.

Works by Henry David Thoreau
and Nathaniel Hawthorne
are in the public domain.

Graphic Design and Editing:
Nancy Richardot Tenney
Concord Graphic Design
Editing:
Amy Noel Wyman
John H.L. Bingham

Printing, Binding and Color Separations:
The Nimrod Press
Westwood, Massachusetts

Photography credits appear on page 72

Preface

My first visit to Concord, in 1947, was to visit Mary Winder Crocker who was a student at Concord Academy. We were married two years later and moved to Concord in the spring of 1950 after my graduation from Harvard College. Our first home was a small cabin in the woods on top of Punkatasset Hill, leased from Mr. Gordon Hutchins. Although we had running water and a wood burning stove, we had no electricity. Our light was from candles and our heat and hot water from the wood burning stove. It was this wonderful, spartan living that gave us a lasting appreciation of the simple life and the natural beauty of Concord. As winter approached, we moved to Lang Street, where in December, the first of our five children was born.

In 1956, to better accommodate our expanding family, we built our own house on a five-acre parcel on Barnes Hill Road. Our next door neighbors for many years were the Emerson family. It is through David Emerson was a great-grandson of Ralph Waldo Emerson, that we came to know of the self-reliant lifestyle of the Emerson tradition. Our children knew many of the eight Emerson children as young playmates. Although the Emersons moved away some time ago, we still keep in touch with the family through Danny Emerson, one of the Emerson children who visits with us from time to time.

After living in Concord for forty-five years, I have become joyfully rooted in the wonderful tradition and beauty of Concord. As a consequence, I feel inspired to share with others some of the delightful images that my wife and I have come to appreciate over the years. Coinciding with this urge to share Concord's beauty was a desire to learn more about Concord's famous literary circle.

What follows is a collage of Concord's enduring natural beauty blended with words from four of Concord's famous "poets": Ralph Waldo Emerson, Henry David Thoreau, Louisa May Alcott, and Nathaniel Hawthorne. These four are Concord's literary group, those who lived, wrote, and were buried here. These authors have enriched the lives of countless people around the world, national leaders and private citizens alike. I hope through this blending of text and images the reader will discover subliminal glimpses of the "transcendental", the simple philosophy of life spawned by these four writers of the nineteenth century.

Acknowledgments

I am most grateful to Nancy Tenney for her enthusiasm and patience in helping me publish this book. Her design skills and editorial prowess were essential for the completion of this project. She was ably assisted in editing by Amy Noel Wyman of Concord and John Bingham of Lincoln. Special thanks are extended to Marcia Moss of the Concord Free Public Library, Jan Turnquist, and Tom Blanding for their assistance in reviewing the historical facts of the biographies contained herein. Also, I want to thank Danny Emerson for referring me to Leslie Morris at the Houghton Library, which held the rights to the Ralph Waldo Emerson papers. And, finally, I want to thank my wife, Murry, for her assistance in selecting photographs for this book and help editing the text.

Introduction

Concord. The name evokes memories of our country's history, as well as the great literary heritage so embodied in Concord's own poets and writers. Let us begin our journey in Concord's colonial past, before its "Transcendentalists" blossomed, by visiting with the Reverend William Emerson, first owner of the famous Old Manse, and grandfather of Ralph Waldo Emerson.

Reverend William Emerson arrived in 1765 to be pastor of the Church in Concord. In 1766, he married Phebe Bliss, the former pastor's daughter, and started construction of the Manse. William Emerson preached for liberty and against the oppression of England. Concord rallied for action and in 1774 the Town voted to fund the company of young "minute men"—ready to fight at a moment's notice. In October of that year, Emerson was invited by the Provincial Congress in Concord to be its Chaplain.

After the battles at Concord and Lexington, Emerson served the troops in Cambridge. Thus his career had shifted from parish minister to military chaplain. His final post was with the Continental Army at Fort Ticonderoga, New York, where he contracted camp fever and died at the age of thirty-three in Rutland, Vermont before he could reach home. His body lies buried there in an unmarked grave. The Town of Concord raised a monument to him in 1826.

Widowed in 1776, young Phebe Bliss Emerson and her five children stayed on in the Manse. In 1780, she married Ezra Ripley, minister of the Concord church. Reverend Ripley was as devoted to her Emerson children as he was to the three children they had together. This support extended to her grandchildren, one of whom was Ralph Waldo Emerson. The relationship between Ralph Waldo Emerson and his step-grandfather began after Ralph's father's death in 1811 when, at the age of nearly eight, Ralph Waldo accompanied his mother and siblings to the Manse for an extended stay.

Phebe Bliss Emerson Ripley, mistress of the Manse, passed away in 1825. Nine years later, in 1834, Ezra Ripley fulfilled his promise to the Emerson descendants, once again inviting Ralph Waldo Emerson and his mother to join him to live in the Manse. That was the year Emerson began writing his first book, *Nature.* The following year, in September 1835, he purchased a house on the Cambridge Turnpike and moved in with his new bride, Lydia Jackson.

In 1840, seven-year-old Louisa May Alcott and her family moved to Concord, into the Hosmer Cottage on Main Street. Her father, Amos Bronson Alcott, had been attracted to Concord by his friendship with Ralph Waldo Emerson. The Alcott family also lived at Hillside (later Hawthorne's Wayside) and Orchard House. Alcott and his wife, Abigail, encouraged their daughters to expand their minds and make use of their natural talents. Louisa's writing career began with magazine work, short stories and an unprofitable novel, *Moods.* She then insured the family's financial security with the success of *Little Women* when it was published in 1868. Hers is a story of courage and persistence in the face of many challenges.

Two years after the Alcotts arrived in Concord, Nathaniel Hawthorne became the second famous author to take up residence in the Manse. He leased it from Ezra Ripley's son, Samuel, and his wife, Sarah. Hawthorne moved in on his wedding day, July 9, 1842, with his bride, Sophia Peabody. It was there that Hawthorne came to know and admire Emerson and is believed to have written *Mosses from an Old Manse,* a collection of stories, essays, and reveries published in 1846. Since that time, the house is referred to as the "Old Manse."

In 1845, Henry David Thoreau built a one-room house at Walden Pond on the land of his friend Ralph Waldo Emerson. In Thoreau's words, "I went to the woods because I wished to live deliberately, to front only the essential facts of life, and see if I could not learn what it had to teach, and not, when I came to die, discover that I had not lived." He stayed over two years, living and writing "a mile from any neighbor." Thoreau was an individualist, with a strong personality, plain-spoken, and caring little for conventional ways. His closest friends were Emerson, Ellery Channing, and the Alcott family.

Most historians agree that Ralph Waldo Emerson greatly influenced the creation of a strong literary movement in Concord in the early to mid-eighteen-eighties. He enjoyed surrounding himself with gifted individuals, and he respected their genius. They in turn admired his new ideas and his basic philosophy on nature and man. The group of friends, Emerson, Bronson Alcott, and Thoreau were catalysts for each other both personally and in their work. They were called and are considered Transcendentalists, and along with Hawthorne and Louisa May Alcott are recognized as the core of Concord's literary group. Concord also has other famous American writers to her credit, including Margaret Fuller, William Ellery Channing, Franklin B. Sanborn, George William Curtis, Jane Austin, and Margaret Sidney. All have made an indelible impression on Concord past and present and will always continue to influence the essence of Concord's future. ◆

Louisa May Alcott

Louisa May Alcott, born on November 29, 1832, in Germantown, Pennsylvania, grew up in Boston and Concord. Her father, Amos Bronson Alcott, was an eccentric, but brilliant writer and thinker, and a great friend of Ralph Waldo Emerson. Louisa received most of her education from her father who, at one time, ran the Temple School in Boston. She was an exuberant child with a willful personality, often spending hours wandering the wharves or driving her hoop around Boston Common. Though young Louisa was the family tomboy, she had a penchant for writing stories and poems.

After several moves in and around Boston, the family settled in Concord to be near Ralph Waldo Emerson. Their first home was Hosmer Cottage, complete with an acre of land, where Bronson Alcott would garden, educate his girls, and give Conversations. Later at Hillside, now known as Wayside, Louisa spent her early teenage years. It was this family time, growing up with her three sisters, that formed the basis for her most notable achievement, *Little Women*, published in 1868. In 1858, the Alcotts had moved to the famous Orchard House, now a museum.

Louisa was by nature duty-bound to her family. As a young woman, she made up her mind to forego marriage in favor of a writing career that might help her family make ends meet. She sold her first story at sixteen, then followed her intense interest in theater, writing several melodramatic plays, none of which were ever produced. Her later poems and short stories were moderately successful. And, by 1860, these works were appearing in the *Atlantic Monthly* magazine. She had chosen public over private life— through her books she promoted a new order of family life, engendered by her parents and their transcendental friends.

In 1862, volunteering as an army nurse in the Civil War, Louisa served the Union Hospital in George-town. But, a severe attack of typhoid and pneumonia forced her to give up nursing. She said, "I was never sick a day in my life before thirty and never had a day of good health after." Upon her return home, she wrote *Hospital Sketches* about her Civil War experiences. Her first novel, *Moods*, was not successful. When approached by a publisher to write a girls' book, Louisa was not enthusiastic, yet she had always wanted to write about her family. *Little Women* was published in 1868, bringing her success and her family financial security. The book is a revealing portrait of a unique family, where daughters were taught to live a life of self-actualization as well as service. *Little Women* is still widely read and appreciated the world over.

Louisa was fortunate to have two brilliant mentors—Ralph Waldo Emerson and Henry David Thoreau. She would visit Emerson in his study and had access to his library. Thoreau would take the Alcott girls berry picking and rowing on Walden Pond. As she grew older, she filled her life with pioneering reform activities, from anti-slavery to women's suffrage. "I can remember when Anti-slavery was in just the same state that Suffrage is now, and take more pride in the very small help we Alcotts could give than in all the books I ever wrote or ever shall write."

Louisa May Alcott stood firm in her beliefs throughout her life. Her ability to express these experiences authentically resonated deeply with her readers. This is well- illustrated in two of her lesser known poems—one to Thoreau, *Thoreau's Flute*, and one to her father. On March 6, 1888, Louisa died at the age of fifty-five, and lies buried in Sleepy Hollow Cemetery. ◆

Ralph Waldo Emerson

Ralph Waldo Emerson was born in Boston on May 25, 1803. His father, Reverend William Emerson, was a congregational minister, pastor of the First Church of Boston. Ralph was frail and undersized as a youth, and preferred reading to play.

Due to his father's strong emphasis on education, Emerson advanced quickly and entered Harvard College at age fourteen, graduating at eighteen. He received no honors, however, because he preferred to read what interested him rather than what was assigned.

After Harvard, Emerson taught school for three years, saved his earnings, and entered Cambridge Divinity School. In 1826, he began to preach, and in 1829 was ordained, becoming the minister of a large Unitarian Church in Boston. After only three years, however, he left the ministry, due to philosophical differences.

In 1834, Emerson, then a widower, moved with his mother into the Manse in Concord to live with his step-grandfather, Ezra Ripley. On September 14, 1835, at thirty-two, Emerson married Lydia Jackson and moved from the Manse to their new home on Cambridge Turnpike. Here he lived out his long and productive life.

One of Emerson's major works was the book, *Nature,* the first statement of his basic philosophy. Its aim was to celebrate the unity between God, the soul, and nature. Written largely in the Manse, it sold only a few copies when published in 1836, but later it became the bible of the Transcendentalists and enjoyed wide acclaim in England when it was supported by Thomas Carlyle.

The essays of Emerson had a powerful influence on the people of his own generation, and on later generations around the world. "Self-Reliance," which stressed knowing and trusting one's self, particularly inspired the young people of his time. To this day, Emerson is regarded as one of the most revered writers of American thought.

Emerson also wrote poetry—although he is known more for the ideas portrayed than for his talent as a poet. "The Rhodora" might be an exception, one of Emerson's most artfully-written poems.

Ralph Waldo Emerson lived simply. He derived much of his inspiration and thought from his daily walks through Concord's woods and fields. As did other great thinkers, he presented his philosophies on lecture tours across America, which was an arduous undertaking in his time. His pioneering ideas often shocked the conservative populace. His approach was simply to state new ideas, not to criticize the prevailing attitudes of the day.

Emerson participated in Concord's life, not shying away like Thoreau and Hawthorne. He sat on committees and spoke to all with respect, even though most were less educated than he. He knew he lacked skill with his hands and admired the tradespeople around him. Although some of his thoughts and ideas were controversial in conservative Concord, such as his view against slavery, eventually the townspeople supported him. Personally, he was always respected and beloved.

Emerson died on April 27, 1882, after a short illness and lies buried in Sleepy Hollow Cemetery. ◊

Nathaniel Hawthorne

Nathaniel Hawthorne was born in Salem, Massachusetts, in 1804, the son of an aristocratic but impoverished sea captain. His family and community, steeped in tradition, raised him in a puritanical atmosphere.

Nathaniel's father died when the boy was four years old. His grief-stricken mother withdrew into a lonely world of her own, not even taking meals with her children. When he was nine, young Nathaniel broke his foot. He was confined to the house for two years, with only his books and his sister for companionship. The boy developed a shyness and reserve that he never overcame. At fourteen he spent a year in the wilderness of Sebago Lake, Maine, an experience that gave him an intimate appreciation of nature and an increased love of solitude.

Nathaniel graduated from Bowdoin College in 1825, then returned to Salem and lived in near seclusion for almost ten years. Seven years later, he moved to Concord after marrying Sophia Peabody. They settled in the Manse, where they became intimate friends of the Thoreau and Emerson families. They lived a simple, secluded life filled with rustic pleasures such as fishing, swimming, rowing in Thoreau's old boat, gardening, and reading Shakespeare or Milton to each other. The three years in this house gave Nathaniel the inspiration and time to write his first book, *Mosses from the Old Manse.*

Hawthorne could not earn enough through writing to support his family, so he took a position in Salem, in 1845, as a custom surveyor. Back under the influence of Salem's century-old puritanical atmosphere, Hawthorne's thoughts forged *The Scarlet Letter,* the book that made him famous. It was published in 1850 and, as he declared, "Fame was won!"

Other famous novels followed: *The House of the Seven Gables,* and *The Blithedale Romance* (about his Brook Farm experience). He had consistently chosen to emphasize his favorite themes—sin, repentance, and atonement with God. Hawthorne returned to Concord in 1852. At that time he became somewhat more sociable, yet he was still a reserved person, preferring lengthy meditations in nature to life in the center of town.

Nathaniel Hawthorne was asked by presidential-hopeful Franklin Pierce to write his campaign biography. President Pierce then appointed Hawthorne to be the U.S. Consul in Liverpool, England, in 1853. Hawthorne lived in Europe for the next seven years, toured widely and as a result became more cosmopolitan.

His successful days, however, were numbered. He returned to Concord as the conflicts leading to the Civil War were breaking out. The suffering weighed heavily on Hawthorne and he began to fail, not able to complete any of his last books. In May 1864, while traveling with President Pierce in New Hampshire, Hawthorne died in his sleep. He is buried near Thoreau in Sleepy Hollow Cemetery.

Henry David Thoreau

Henry David Thoreau was born in Concord in 1817. After schooling in Concord and at Harvard College, he taught in the Concord public schools, but resigned in protest of the school policy of striking unruly students. He then founded a private, more progressive school with his older brother, John. Thoreau was devoted to his brother and suffered greatly when John died suddenly of lockjaw.

At the age of twenty-seven, in the spring of 1845, Thoreau resolved to live a simpler life. He went to the shores of Walden Pond, on Emerson's land, where with a borrowed ax he built a small one-room house. He moved in on July 4, 1845 and stayed two years, two months and two days, making occasional trips to town. To live off the land, he cleared an area around the house and raised his own vegetables. One of the reasons Thoreau moved to the house at Walden Pond was to memorialize his brother by writing *A Week on the Concord and Merrimack Rivers.* While there, he also wrote the journal that provided the content for his book, *Walden,* or *Life in the Woods,* published in 1854. *Walden* is a compilation of Thoreau's reflections on his time at the pond, a very personal, detailed, peace-filled account of his life and thoughts there. It is the intimate and transcendent quality of this and his other works that makes Thoreau's writings so internationally important and appealing.

Thoreau was deeply socially conscious, as exemplified in his essay "Civil Disobedience" — an inspiration to both Gandhi and Dr. Martin Luther King, Jr. He sought greater freedom for individuals and more chance for them to develop creatively. He spoke out against injustice and convention.

Fond of solitude, Thoreau had few friends, Emerson perhaps being his closest. Emerson summed up Thoreau's life in these words: "He was bred to no profession; he never married; he lived alone; he never went to church; he never voted; he refused to pay a tax to the State; he ate no flesh, he drank no wine, he never knew the use of tobacco, and though a naturalist, he used neither trap nor gun."

At age forty-four, Thoreau died of tuberculosis in Concord in 1862. He is buried on the ridge in Sleepy Hollow Cemetery.

"Every day or two I strolled to the village to hear some of the gossip which is incessantly going on there, circulating either from mouth to mouth, or from newspaper to newspaper, and which, taken in homeopathic doses, was really as refreshing in its way as the rustle of leaves and the peeping of frogs. As I walked in the woods to see the birds and squirrels, so I walked in the village to see the men and boys; instead of the wind among the pines I heard the carts rattle. In one direction from my house there was a colony of muskrats in the river meadow; under the grove of elms and buttonwoods in the other horizon was a village of busy men, as curious to me as if they had been prairie dogs, each sitting at the mouth of its burrow, or running over to a neighbor's to gossip. I went there frequently to observe their habits."

Walden
Henry David Thoreau

Main Street, 1995

Main Street, 1995

Main Street, 1880s

"I indulge in gorgeous fancies and wish that I had dared inscribe them upon my pages and set them before the public. ...How should I dare to interfere with the proper grayness of old Concord? The dear old town has never known a startling hue since the redcoats were there. ...To have had Mr. Emerson for an intellectual god all one's life is to be invested with a chain armor of propriety. ...And what would my own good father think of me?...No, my dear, I shall always be a wretched victim to the respectable traditions of Concord."
Louisa May Alcott

Keyes Barn, off of Liberty Street

First Parish Church, Lexington Road

"Crossing a bare common, in snow puddles, at twilight, under a clouded sky, without having in my thoughts any occurrence of special good fortune, I have enjoyed a perfect exhilaration."

Nature
Ralph Waldo Emerson

Macone's Ice Pond

"I wish to speak a word for Nature, for absolute freedom and wildness, as contrasted with a freedom and culture merely civil, to regard man as inhabitant or a part and parcel of Nature, rather than a member of society."

Walking
Henry David Thoreau

The Old Manse

"How gently, too, did the sight of the Old Manse—best seen from the river, overshadowed with its willows, and all environed about with the foliage of its orchard and avenue—how gently did its gray, homely aspect rebuke the speculative extravagances of the day!

Mosses from the Old Manse
Nathaniel Hawthorne

"It is a curious subject of observation and inquiry whether hatred and love be not the same thing at bottom. Each in its utmost development supposes a high degree of intimacy and heart knowledge; each renders one individual dependent for the food of his affections and spiritual life upon the other; each leaves the passionate lover or no less the passionate hater, forlorn and desolate by the withdrawal of his subject. Philosophically considered, therefore the two passions seem essentially the same, except that one happens to be seen in a celestial radiance, and the other in a dusky and lurid glow. In the spiritual world the old physician and the minister—mutual victims as they have been—may, unawares, have found their earthly stock of hatred and antipathy transmuted into golden love."

The Scarlet Letter
Nathaniel Hawthorne

Wayside

Two Rivers

Ralph Waldo Emerson

Thy summer voice, Musketaquit,
Repeats the music of the rain;
But sweeter rivers pulsing flit
Through thee, as thou through Concord Plain.

Thou in thy narrow banks art pent:
The stream I love unbounded goes
Through flood and sea and firmament;
Through light, through life it forward flows.

I see the inundation sweet,
I hear the spending of the stream
Through years, through men, through nature fleet,
Through love and thought, through power and dream.

Musketaquit, a goblin strong,
Of shard and flint makes jewels gay;
They lose their grief who hear his song,
And where he wings is the day of day.

So forth and brighter fares my stream, —
Who drink it shall not thirst again;
No darkness stains its equal gleam,
And ages drop in it like rain.

Concord River

Concord Hymn

Ralph Waldo Emerson
Sung at the completion of the Battle Monument, July 4, 1837

By the rude bridge that arched the flood,
Their flag to April's breeze unfurled,
Here once the embattled farmers stood
And fired the shot heard round the world.

The foe long since in silence slept;
Alike the conqueror silent sleeps;
And Time the ruined bridge has swept
Down the dark stream which seaward creeps.

On this green bank, by this soft stream,
We set today a votive stone;
That memory their deed redeem,
When, like our sires, our sons are gone.

Spirit, that made those heroes dare
To die, and leave their children free,
Bid Time and Nature gently spare
The shaft we raise to them and thee.

The Old North Bridge

The Concord Minute Man by Daniel Chester French

The Buttrick Mansion, Minuteman National Park Headquarters

Winter at the Bridge

British Soldiers at Patriot's Day Parade

Mock Battle at the Bridge Patriot's Day

The Fenn School Band, Patriot's Day Parade

Fife and Drum Players, Patriot's Day Parade

The Wright Tavern, built 1747

Home of Ralph Waldo Emerson

Squash, McGrath Farm

"Generally, every fruit, on ripening, and just before it falls, when it commences a more independent and individual existence, requiring less nourishment from any source, and that not so much from the earth through its stem as from the sun and air, acquires a bright tint. So do leaves. The physiologist says it is 'due to an increased absorption of oxygen.' That is the scientific account of the matter, – only a reassertion of the fact. But I am more interested in the rosy cheek than I am to know what particular diet the maiden fed on. The very forest and herbage, the pellicle of the earth, must acquire a bright color, an evidence of its ripeness, – as if the globe itself were a fruit on its stem, with ever a cheek toward the sun."

Autumnal Tints
Henry David Thoreau

"October is the month for painted leaves. Their rich glow now flashes round the world. As fruits and leaves and the day itself acquire a bright tint just before they fall, so the year near its setting. October is its sunset sky; November the later twilight."

Autumnal Tints
Henry David Thoreau

"As when the summer comes from the south, the snowbanks melt, and the face of the earth becomes green before it, so shall the advancing spirit create its ornaments along its path, and carry with it the beauty it visits, and the song which enchants it; it shall draw beautiful faces, warm hearts, wise discourse, and heroic acts, around its way, until evil is no more seen. The kingdom of man over nature, which cometh not with observation, – a dominion such as now is beyond his dream of God."

Nature, Ralph Waldo Emerson

Maplewood Farm

Spring still makes spring in the mind
When sixty years are told;
Love wakes anew this throbbing heart,
And we are never old.
Over the winter glaciers
I see the summer glow,
And through the wild-piled snowdrift,
The warm rosebuds below.

Ralph Waldo Emerson

Thoreau's Flute

by Louisa May Alcott

We, sighing, said, "Our Pan is dead;
His pipe hangs mute beside the river;—
Around it wistful sunbeams quiver,
But Music's airy voice is fled.
Spring mourns as for untimely frost;
The bluebird chants a requiem;
The willow-blossom waits for him;—
The Genius of the wood is lost."

Then from the flute, untouched by hands,
There came a low, harmonious breath:
"For such as he there is no death;—
His life the eternal life commands;
Above man's aims his nature rose:
The wisdom of a just content
Made one small spot a continent,
And turned to poetry Life's prose.

Haunting the hills, the stream, the wild,
Swallow and aster, lake and pine
To him grew human or divine, —
Fit mates for this large-hearted child
Such homage Nature ne'er forgets,
And yearly on the coverlid
'Neath which her darling lieth hid
Will write his name in violets. "

To him no vain regrets belong,
Whose soul, that finer instrument,
Gave to the world no poor lament,
But wood-notes ever sweet and strong.
O lonely friend! he still will be
A potent presence, though unseen, —
Steadfast, sagacious, and serene:
Seek not for him, — he is with thee.

September 1863

Sleepy Hollow Cemetery

The Rhodora

Ralph Waldo Emerson

In May, when sea-winds pierced our solitudes,
I found the fresh Rhodora in the woods,
Spreading its leafless blooms in a damp nook,
To please the desert and the sluggish brook.
The purple petals, fallen in the pool,
Made the black water with their beauty gay;

Here might the red-bird come his plumes to cool,
And court the flower that cheapens his array.

Rhodora! if sages ask thee why
This charm is wasted on the earth and sky,
Tell them, dear, that if eyes were made for seeing,
Then Beauty is its own excuse for being:
Why thou wert there, O rival of the rose!
I never thought to ask, I never knew:
But in my simple ignorance, suppose
The self-same Power that brought me there brought you.

"I learned this, at least, by my experiment, that if one advances confidently in the direction of his dreams, and endeavors to live the life of which he has imagined, he will meet with a success unexpected in common hours."

Walden
Henry David Thoreau

"I went to the woods because I wished to live deliberately, to front only the essential facts of life, and see if I could not learn what it had to teach, and not, when I came to die, discover that I had not lived."

Walden
Henry David Thoreau

Walden Pond

"The life in us is like the water in the river. It may rise this year higher than man has ever known it, and flood the parched uplands; even this may be the eventful year, which will drown out all our muskrats. It was not always dry land where we dwell. I see far inland the banks which the stream anciently washed, before science began to record its freshets."

Walden
Henry David Thoreau

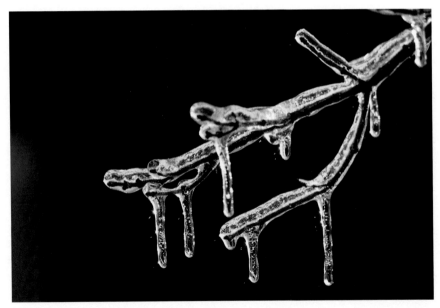

Ice Branch

"I find it wholesome to be alone the greater part of the time. To be in company, even with the best, is soon wearisome and dissipating. I love to be alone. I never found the companion that was so companionable as solitude. We are for the most part more lonely when we go abroad among men than when we stay in our chambers."

Walden, from the chapter Solitude
Henry David Thoreau

Concord River

Concord Independent Battery, established in 1804

Orchard House, home of the Alcotts

"Jo! Jo, where are you?" cried Meg, at the foot of the garret stairs.

"Here!" answered a husky voice from above; and, running up, Meg found her sister eating apples and crying over the *Heir of Redclyffe*, wrapped up in a comforter on an old three-legged sofa by the sunny window. This was Jo's favorite refuge; and here she loved to retire with half a dozen russets and a nice book to enjoy the quiet and the society of a pet rat who lived near by, and didn't mind her a particle.

Little Women
Louisa May Alcott

Little Women

Excerpt from Chapter XIV, Secrets

Louisa May Alcott

"I may get into a scrape for telling; but I didn't promise not to, so I will, for I never feel easy in my mind till I've told you any plummy bit of news I get. I know where Meg's glove is."

" Is that all?" said Jo, looking disappointed, as Laurie nodded and twinkled, with a face full of mysterious intelligence.

" It's quite enough for the present, as you'll agree when I tell you where it is."

" Tell, then."

Laurie bent, and whispered three words in Jo's ear, which produced a comical change. She stood and stared at him for a minute, looking both surprised and displeased, then walked on, saying sharply, "How do you know?"

" Saw it."

" Where?"

" Pocket."

" All this time?"

" Yes; isn't that romantic?"

" No, it's horrid."

" Don't you like it?"

" Of course I don't. It's ridiculous; it won't be allowed. My patience! what would Meg say? "

" You are not to tell anyone; mind that."

" I didn't promise."

" That was understood, and I trusted you."

" Well, I won't for the present, anyway; but I'm disgusted, and wish you hadn't told me."

" I thought you'd be pleased."

" At the idea of anybody coming to take Meg away? No, thank you."

" You'll feel better about it when somebody comes to take you away."

" I'd like to see anyone try it," cried Jo fiercely.

" So should I!" and Laurie chuckled at the idea.

" I don't think secrets agree with me; I feel rumpled up in my mind since you told me that," said Jo rather ungratefully.

" Race down this hill with me, and you'll be all right," suggested Laurie.

No one was in sight; the smooth road sloped invitingly before her; and finding the temptation irresistible, Jo darted away, soon leaving hat and comb behind her, and scattering hair-pins as she ran. Laurie reached the goal first, and was quite satisfied with the success of his treatment; for his Atalanta came panting up, with flying hair, bright eyes, ruddy cheeks, and no signs of dissatisfaction in her face.

" I wish I was a horse; then I could run for miles in this splendid air, and not lose my breath. It was capital; but see what a guy it's made me. Go, pick up my things, like a cherub as you are," said Jo, dropping down under a maple tree, which was carpeting the bank with crimson leaves.

Laurie leisurely departed to recover the lost property, and Jo bundled up her braids, hoping no one would pass by till she was tidy again. But someone did pass, and who should it be but Meg, looking particularly ladylike in her state and festival suit, for she had been making calls.

" What in the world are you doing here?" she asked, regarding her dishevelled sister with well-bred surprise.

" Getting leaves," meekly answered Jo, sorting the rosy handful she had just swept up.

" And hair-pins," added Laurie throwing half a dozen into Jo's lap. " They grow on this road, Meg; so do combs and brown straw hats."

" You have been running, Jo; how could you? When *will* you stop such romping ways?" said Meg reprovingly, as she settled her cuffs, and smoothed her hair, with which the wind had taken liberties.

" Never till I'm stiff and old, and have to use a crutch. Don't try to make me grow up before my time, Meg: it's hard enough to have you change all of a sudden; let me be a little girl as long as I can."

As she spoke, Jo bent over the leaves to hide the trembling of her lips; for lately she had felt that Margaret was fast getting to be a woman, and Laurie's secret made her dread the separation which must surely come some time, and now seemed very near. He saw the trouble in her face and drew Meg's attention from it by asking quickly, " Where have you been calling, all so fine?"

"At the Gardiners', and Sallie has been telling me all about Belle Moffat's wedding. It was very splendid, and they have gone to spend the winter in Paris. Just think how delightful that must be!"

" Do you envy her, Meg?" said Laurie.

" I'm afraid I do."

" I'm glad of it!" muttered Jo, tying on her hat with a jerk.

" Why?" asked Meg, looking surprised.

" Because if you care much about riches, you will never go and marry a poor man," said Jo, frowning at Laurie who was mutely warning her to mind what she said.

" I shall never '*go* and marry' any one," observed Meg, walking on with great dignity, while the others followed, laughing, whispering, skipping stones and "behaving like children," as Meg said to herself, though she might have been tempted to join them if she had not had her best dress on.

"Notwithstanding, the red maple is the most intense scarlet of any of our trees, the sugar maple has been the most celebrated, and Michaux in his 'Sylva' does not speak of the autumnal color of the former. About the second of October, these trees, both large and small, are most brilliant, though many are still green. In 'sprout-lands' they seem to vie with one another, and ever some particular one in the midst of the crowd will be of a peculiarly pure scarlet, and by its more intense color attract our eye even at a distance, and carry off the palm. A large red maple swamp, when at the height of its change, is the most obviously brilliant of all tangible things, where I dwell, so abundant is this tree with us. It varies much both in form and color. A great many are merely yellow; more, scarlet; others, scarlet deepening into crimson, more red than common. Look at yonder swamp of maples mixed with pines, at the base of a pine-clad hill, a quarter of a mile off, so that you get the full effect of the bright colors, without detecting the imperfections of the leaves, and see their yellow, scarlet, and crimson fires, of all tints mingled and contrasted with the green."

Autumnal Tints
Henry David Thoreau

Hosta in the Morning Dew

"Lastly, in lieu of these shifting scenes, came back the rude market-place of the Puritan settlement, with all the townspeople assembled and levelling their stern regards at Hester Prynne, — yes, at herself, — who stood on the scaffold of the pillory, and infant on her arm, and the letter A, in scarlet, fantastically embroidered with gold-thread, upon her bosom!

Could it be true? She clutched the child so fiercely to her breast, that it set forth a cry; she turned her eyes downward at the scarlet letter, and even touched it with her finger, to assure herself that the infant and the shame were real. Yes! — these were her realities, — all else had vanished!

Scarlet Letter
Nathaniel Hawthorne

Great Meadows

"The sun sets on some retired meadow, where no house is visible, with all the glory and splendor that it lavishes on cities, and perchance as it has never set before,–where there is but a solitary marsh hawk to have his wings gilded by it, or only a musquash looks out from his cabin, and there is some little black-veined brook in the midst of the marsh, just beginning to meander, winding slowly round a decaying stump. We walked in so pure and bright a light, gilding the withered grass and leaves, so softly and serenely bright, I thought I had never bathed in such a golden flood, without a ripple or a murmur to it. The west side of every wood and rising ground gleamed like the boundary of Elysium, and the sun on our backs seemed like a gentle herdsman driving us home at evening."

Walking
Henry David Thoreau

"In the woods, we return to reason and faith. There I feel nothing can befall me in life, —no disgrace, no calamity, (leaving me my eyes,) which nature cannot repair. Standing on the bare ground, — my head bathed by the blithe air, and uplifted into infinite space, —all mean egotism vanishes. I become a transparent eye-ball; I am nothing; I see all: the currents of the Universal Being circulate through me; I am part or parcel of God."

Nature
Ralph Waldo Emerson

Bibliography

1. French, Allen. *Historic Concord and the Lexington Fight* Concord Free Public Library,
    2nd revised edition, 1992.

2. Sherman, David E. and Redlich, Rosemarie. *Literary America* Dodd, Mead & Co.,
    1952.

3. Stern, Madeleine. *Louisa May Alcott* University of Oklahoma Press, 1950.

Credits:

Photographs on pages 23, 39, 65, 70, and the back cover are by Mary Winder Nordblom.

Main Street Concord 1880 (page 23) included with the permission of the Concord Free Public Library.

All other photographs are by Rodger P. Nordblom.

The Old Manse, page 28, is owned and managed by The Trustees of Reservations and held in the Public Trust.

Orchard House, page 59, included with the permission of The Louisa May Alcott Memorial Association.

Terns @ Chillaw Sand Spits **HdeS

Gull biled tern @ Chillaw Sandspits **HdeS

SERENDIPITY
OF WILDERNESS

HARENDRA DE SILVA | LAKKUMAR FERNANDO | SANDUN DE SILVA

Guest Photographs By

Palitha Anthony
LJ Mendis Wickremasinghe
Uditha Hettige
Ifham Raji

Consulting Editor
Lester Perera

Layout and Editing
Warna Perera

WHY ANOTHER BOOK ON WILDLIFE? AUTHOR'S COMMENTS

Harendra de Silva - HdeS

Why did a relatively old paediatrician who started birding late in life want to do a book on wild life? Firstly I did not realize what I had missed in life till I was fifty! I want to make a point that it is never too late to enjoy nature. As a professional I was really busy building my academic life and earning for an insecure future! The excuse I and many other professionals have is "we are too busy"! I believe that in spite of a busy schedule you can have a weekend here and there to enjoy the unknown and unexpected behavior of birds and animals. In addition, when I was distraught trying to do things for children after the tsunami during the time I was the chairman of the National Child Protection Authority, taking pictures of birds and looking at them kept me sane (if I was sane before!). The word 'serendipity' although hacked since recently, has been classified as one of the most difficult 10 words in English to give a meaning. 'Pleasant surprise, 'unexpected finding' are some of the meanings given. At the same time Serendib was the name used by Arabs for Sri Lanka and therefore has relevance, since all these photographs were taken in Sri Lanka. One of the most revealing aspects was to understand bird behavior including courting, raring, feeding and protection of babies which is close to the heart of Paediatricians. We have tried to venture into some aspects of the science of mainly birds for laymen to understand

LakKumar Fernando - LF

I was into some wild life but largely it was about watching elephants for a long time. Few years ago the areas to watch elephants became smaller every day with terrorist activity in most natural reserves. Switching to birds was a good fall back option at that time, but unlike the elephants who allow us to enjoy seeing them for hours, birds were disappearing from sight within seconds and taking a photo became a 'must' for me. However without any doubt it was none other than my teacher in the medical faculty and boss at the Children's ward of Karapitiya Hospital, Prof Harendra de Silva who took me to both birds and to somewhat serious wildlife photography. I remember how he hand carried my first DSLR camera and the lens weighing several kilos he bought in US. It was a not so common situation of a student-teacher turning into 'friends' doing some wildlife photography together. The nature of Prof's personality was such I did not feel uncomfortable doing such photographic trips together. The biggest problem I had was to be in touch with my ward while in the jungle. Though my trips were on days I was officially not on-call to the ward I was sure to get calls from my juniors on these 'off' days too. I always carried several telephones with different networks that give different coverage. I was sure to stop at known spots in the wild life places that has some mobile signals to look for call alerts and SMSs especially for my unofficial 'dengue hotline'. Few times the calls came at bad times and I lost some great opportunities, but this was not unexpected.

Sandun de Silva - SdeS

I am Prof Harendra's eldest son and is a a qualified chef but took to photography after I picked one of my father's old cameras to photograph dishes for magazines, and everyone realized my artistic eye as a photographer and is now a well-known fashion and architectural photographer.

Other Invited Contributors

Since this book is dedicated to Dr. T.S.U de Zylva, it was appropriate to invite other photographers with varied interests to pay tribute to this outstanding photographer. On the other hand it was difficult to invite many people because of cost. Therefore the decision to invite good friends who also have other interests such as mammals, reptiles, amphibians and endemics was made. It also significantly helps to fill some of the gaps in variety.

Palitha Anthony - PA
LJ Mendis Wickremasinghe - MW
Uditha Hettige - UH
Ifham Raji - IR

Picture Editors **Sandun de Silva** and **Warna Perera**
Layout and Design **Warna Perera**

Lester Perera is acknowledged as a great encyclopedia of birds and wildlife, guide, artist, advisor and a great friend

Dedicated to

Sri Lanka's Foremost and Greatest Bird and Wildlife Photographer of all time

Dr T.S.Upendra de Zylva

Dr. Upendra de Zylva (TSU) was born in Kurunegala in 1927. A son of a pioneer Medical Practitioner in Kurunegala, had his primary education at Maliyadeva College and then went to Royal College Colombo. He was boarded at JP Obeysekera's residence and had to move to Kandy where he had to go to Dharmaraja College. He sat for the last London Matriculation exam which he qualified without much effort and was eligible to do the Colombo University entrance. He then entered the Medical College. He was the first Medico to take a photograph in the operating theatre of a famous surgeon while operating for which he received a Rs 300/- gift which was huge considering the price of film which was only 3 Rs at the time. His interest in photography and Biology continued and was an avid reader of the relevant topics. During a vacation in India his mother bought him a Zeiss Contax camera that resulted in him taking some colour slides of Indian scenes, architecture and people.

When he qualified in 1953 as a doctor his father bought him a 16 mm Bolex Cine Camera which enabled him to venture into movies. After his father's demise in 1954 he joined his brother in law's practice and produced three, 16 mm cines movies: At the Water's Edge, The World in my garden and The Dry Zone Wilderness. He joined the Wild Life and Nature Protection Society and quickly became the District Representative and was soon elected to the General Committee and his work was published in the Loris Magazine. In the early seventies he became a close friend of Dr. Victor Hasselblad and remained a close friend of Dr. Hasselblad untill his death in 1978. He was also elected a member of the Research Committee set up by Dr. Hasselblad. The relatives and friend's donated to the Victor Hasselblad Trust that set up the Turtle Hatchery in Kosgoda. He also received funds following the tsunami to repair the Kosgoda Hatchery. He was also the president of the WNPS and his interest in Wild Life has not waned in spite of getting on in years.

Books published by him include, Birds of Sri Lanka, Jungle Profiles, Images of Birds, Wings in the Wetlands, Birds within Camera Reach, Field Guide to the Birds of Sri Lanka, Sinharaja Rainforest, Cradles on the Sand (in press).

Pied Kingfisher @ Thalangama Tank **LF

ISBN 978-955-95257-2-1

Published by :
Harendra De Silva, LakKumar Fernando and Sandun de Silva
harendra51@gmail.com

Cover page: **Brown-headed Barbet**, nesting on a charred jack tree **HdeS

Printed by Gunaratne Offset (PVT) Ltd

The male **Peafowl** Is invariably the one, that is most photographed. Unfortunately gender discrimination is difficult to avoid since it is the male makeup that is attractive. @ Wilpattu **LF

Indian Peafowl. A male, showing the chestnut primaries adding more colour to the already flamboyant plumage. A common sight seen in most sanctuaries, sometimes start rummaging on domestic garbage. The mournful cry puts off fans and is considered to bring bad luck! It is also the Hindu God Kadiragamar's chariot which makes people revere it from another point and probably prevent them from slaughtering it for meat; preventing extinction!. @ Uda walawe .**HdeS

Black Bulbul, sub species specific to Sri Lanka and Western Ghats, is treated as separate species by some authors. @ Kithulgala **LF

Common Iora. During the breeding season, mainly after the monsoons, the male performs an acrobatic courtship display, darting up into the air fluffing up all his feathers, especially those on the pale green rump, then spiraling down to the original perch. Once he lands, he spreads his tail and droops his wings. @ Kithulgala **LF

Black-naped Monarch Male feeding chicks, it is insectivorous, often hunting by flycatching. It was a difficult task to catch it in the rush, to photograph the yet another uncommon Oriental Dwarf Kingfisher!. Sisira's Rest @ Kitulgala. **LF

4

The uneasy **Forest Wagtail** a migrant is difficult to photograph, as one may imagine from it's name. @ Gampaha **LF

Tissamaharama. 2010 **SdeS

Ruwanwelisaya **SdeS

Abhayagiriya **SdeS

Striated Heron. Negombo lagoon. I was having tea at a restaurant when I saw the bird sliding down. A quick series of pictures at high speed and the pictures tell the rest of the story.
@ Negombo. **LF

Mother's Milk is the Best for babies! Both the Mother and Baby knows the breast feeding code. well. @ Minneriya. **LF

"Come for a fight" or is it just a 'show' like in WWF?. @ Minneriya. **LF

Elephants are notorious for protection of their offspring. The mother was agitated when we got closer, she trumpeted several times, picked grass and threw it on her head while stamping the ground...

...In the meantime the older sibling, a Tusker, grabbed the baby towards it's body with the trunk and prevented the baby from venturing towards us. @ Uda Walawe. **HdeS

Sri Lankan Leopard. @ Yala **HdeS

Sri Lankan Leopard. @ Wilpattu. – Somewhat shy after decades of isolation during the civil war **LF

Orange-billed Babbler (Juvenile) an endemic is similar to the common yellow billed babbler except for colour of the bill plumage and size, with a preference for rainforests of the wet zone as well as cloud forests of the higher hills. It is a noisy bird, and the presence of a large flock may generally be known at some distance by the continual chattering, squeaking and chirping @ Kitulgala. **LF

Yellow-billed Babbler a common garden bird in small flocks often considered unworthy of publication! They are referred to as 'seven sisters' because of it's nature of caring for the brood including nesting, feeding and warding off threats. (Allocaring)

However, a brawl between two flocks was unbelievable, reminiscent of boy's primary school brawl! They are territorial. @ Thalangama. **Hde S

Indian Golden Jackal. The craftiness and viciousness is written all over the face. @ Wilpattu **LF

Zitting Cisticola. A small bird found mainly in grasslands. Males have a zigzagging flight display accompanied by regular "zitting" calls that has been likened to repeated snips of a scissor. @ Habarana **LF

A fascinating display of brisk acrobatics, by **Long-snouted Spinner Dolphin**, on board the Navy ship off Galle harbor, on a whale and dolphin watching cruise. They were following a small fishing boat with a net. It is known that Dolphins cooperate with local fishermen by driving fish into their nets and eating the fish that escape. Dolphins often work as a team to harvest fish schools.

Dolphins search for prey primarily using echolocation, which is similar to sonar. All cetaceans emit clicking sounds and listen for the return echoes to determine the location and shape of nearby items, including potential prey. Their considerable intelligence has driven interaction with humans. They are seen with whales in the Southern and Western Coast from Mirissa and Kalpitiya from November to April. Trincomalee is the place from May to October. **HdeS

Woolly-necked Stork. A suspicious look all round, akin to Thompson and Thomson of Tin Tin fame. @ Polonnaruwa**LF

Adam's Peak, 2011 **SdeS

Bundala, 2007 **SdeS

23

A nesting, **Emerald Dove**, male, what a beautiful sight. @ Kitulgala. **LF

Sri Lanka Green Pigeon an Endemic bird. @ Yala. **HdeS

An **Indian Pond Heron** lying in wait for a frog that was around. We got fed up and gave up after about an hour, but he didn't! With its weight the lotus leaf got filled gradually and sank, he then jumped to an adjoining leaf and kept on repeating the process. @ Debaraweva. **HdeS

Two **Indian Pond Herons** fighting for a fish. @ Yala **HdeS

The frontal featherless shield in **Common Coot's** gives rise to the expression "as bald as a coot," which has been documented to be in use as early as 1430's. Some Coots have difficulty feeding a large family as many as 9 on tiny shrimp and insects that they collect. After a few days they start attacking their own chicks ('Child Abuse') when they beg for food. These attacks are mostly on the weaker chicks, that finally give up begging and die of starvation. At times they drown the chicks. (Life of Birds, David Attenborough) @ Thalangama. **LF

Purple Swamphen, a common bird, but has a great shade of purplish blue; looks like a large blue sapphire adorned with a smaller Ruby. @ Thalangama tank. **HdeS.

Mating Birds @ Thalangama tank **LF

Rosy Starlings. Is a strong migrant, and winters in India and tropical Asia. It is often seen in huge flocks sometimes referred to as eruptions, due to its erratic increase in numbers. @ Bundala. **HdeS

Indian Darters are able to absorb water into its feathers to reduce buoyancy in the underwater expeditions to fish with its spear like beak and the 'spring loaded' long tortuous neck to stab the fish at lightning speed. It has to hang its feathers out to dry by keeping the wings outstretched like its cousin the cormorant. @ Bundala. **HdeS

A male **Northern Pintail** Duck announcing to the females around "Remember who rules around here!". @ Mannar lagoon. The Northern Pintail has been called the "nomads of the skies" due to their wide-ranging migrations. It is probably one of the most hunted ducks! When you do an internet search, most websites advertise "decoys" for pintail duck hunters! No wonder it is classified as "of least concern"on the IUCN Red List. How long will the status last? **HdeS

Little Grebe. Quite common, squirting water high and wide with it's inbuilt Jacuzzi bath, is an excellent swimmer and diver and pursues its fish and aquatic invertebrate prey underwater. When they dive they don't surface for a long time and may come up far away from the original position. @ Thalangama Tank. **HdeS

Cotton Pygmy Goose, in a highly ritualistic courting behavior the male demonstrated his masculinity for a considerable time dancing and chasing behind the female @ Anevilundawa. **HdeS

Cotton Pygmy Goose trying to initiate a courtship. The dark greenish winged bird is the male. @ Anevilundawa. HdeS**

It is the smallest waterfowl, the bill is short and deep at the base, and is goose-like, hence the name.

Pheasant-tailed Jacana a very common water bird turns very attractive in breeding plumage. @ Anewilundawa **LF

Common Moorhen, a species widely distributed around the world. It is known for its aggression in protecting territory. Altruistic behavior by some juveniles of the previous broods (about 3 per year) has been described since they help in the feeding of the new, thereby reducing the burden of parents finding food, which in turn increases the chances of survival. @ Thalangama Tank **LF

Lester and Palitha gave the information about these **Oystercatchers** at the Chillaw Sandspits. It was most difficult to photograph these elusive rare migrants that have not been seen there for years till this year at the time of compiling the book (2012) in Chillaw. I had to often advance by crawling in spite of 3 (later found to have 6) slipped discs and came back on 3 weekends to watch them. LakKumar had not taken up serious photography then and was a paediatrician in Chillaw who came along and these birds I am sure inspired him to become a serious birder. **HdeS

Having heard of the arrivals in 2012, LakKumar was determined to photograph them in Chilaw and this was taken in November 2012. Most **Oystercatchers** are monogamous, although there are reports of polygamy. There is strong mate and site fidelity in the species that have been studied, with one record of a pair defending the same site for 20 years. Could this be the same pair that came in 2006? Oystercatchers are also sometimes known to practice "egg dumping." Like the cuckoo, they sometimes lay their eggs in the nests of other species such as seagulls, abandoning them to be raised by those birds. **LF

Newly hatched, **Red-wattled Lapwing** being cleaned by the sibling born a couple of hours earlier. The ability to run the moment they are born is known as 'precocial' (chicks). They have a longer incubation period, a large proportion of yolk, and the remaining of which gets absorbed before birth from the stomach and the fat gets stored in the liver and under the skin as reserves to fall back in case they cannot forage enough for themselves. The Adult Lapwings are very protective of the babies with any threat it covers the new under the breast, although they play little role in feeding since the chicks forage for themselves. @ Ragama Medical Faculty. **HdeS

Red-wattled Lapwing. "Birds pinpoint the source of a sound by assessing the time lag between it's arrival at either side of the head. Because of the time factor, it is easier to locate a series of sounds rather than one continuous note. This probably explains why the alarm call given by many birds when a predator is near is a pure tone, with a gradual beginning and end, and not a position betraying series of rapid notes, protecting the young, under the wings when a threat such as a crow is heard or seen. They also utter a noise that warns the chicks wandering by, to hit the ground and crouch down. **HdeS

Crouching chicks just after the adult call. **HdeS

Yellow-wattled Lapwing, seen in dry lowlands – Looks like a prop forward in the pack in rugby in this picture (except for the scraggy legs!). Unlike its louder cousin, the Red-wattled Lapwing, the yellow version is less demonstrative and noisy. Parents may visit water and wet their breast feathers ("belly soaking") which then maybe used to cool the eggs or chicks on a hot day. Like its cousin the Red-wattled Lapwing the young are well camouflaged as they forage with the parents and the chicks squat flat on the ground and freeze when parents emit an alarm call. @ Bundala. **HdeS

The **Indian Thick-knee** was classified previously as Eurasian Thick-knee, or Indian Stone-curlew. Whatever the partner said has obviously ruffled its feathers @ Bundala HdeS

"The one that got away!" **Asian Openbill**.

The gap in the bill gives an impression that the fish will get away! In fact they feast mostly on snails and other molluscs. It first pins down the snail with the upper mandible and then uses the sharp tip of the lower mandible like a knife to sever the muscle of the snail from its shell. @ Bundala. **HdeS

Tossing a 'peeled' snail in the process of swallowing.

Haputhale, 2012 **SdeS

Eurasian Kingfisher, it is not as common as the white throated in Sri Lanka. Preening it's feathers after a dip in the Thalangama Tank. **HdeS

Preening is an important way for bird's to groom its feathers to keep them in the finest state. While preening, birds will remove dust, dirt and parasites from its feathers and align each feather in the optimal position in relation to nearby feathers and body shape. Most birds will preen many times a day to keep themselves in a good state. The uropygial gland, or preen gland, is an essential part of preening for most birds. This gland is found near the base of the tail and produces an oily substance, that helps waterproofing feathers and keep them flexible. A bird will typically transfer preen oil to its body during preening by rubbing its beak and head against the gland opening and then rubbing the accumulated oil on the feathers of the body and wings, and on the feet and legs. It appears that the waterproofing effect is not primarily by the uropygiols – although it is hydrophobic – but by an electrostatic charge to the oiled feather through the mechanical action of preening It is also thought that at least in some birds the preen oil contains Vitamin D precursor and that it has anti parasitic (lice) activity Some birds like owls, pigeons, parrots and hawks lack preen glands and instead have specialized feathers that disintegrate into powder down, which serves the same purpose as preen oil. Others may sand bathe or "ant" themselves by rubbing formic acid of ants to clean the feathers and repel parasites.

Stork-billed Kingfisher the largest Kingfisher in Sri Lanka @ Negombo **LF

Pied Kingfisher, It first 'thrashes' the prey on a hard object like a branch (inset) before it swallows always head first. If it does swallow the tail first it would choke with the unfolding (opening) of the tail, fins and scales pointing backwards. @ Hotel Ranweli, Negombo , Boat Safari . **HdeS

07:52:37 AM　　07:52:31 AM　　07:52:28 AM　　07:52:22 AM　　07:52:20 AM　　07:52:17 AM

Elegantly dressed in a widow's "mourning garb", The **Pied Kingfisher** with a tuft of feathers on its head, it hovers over water scanning for fish and plunges vertically downwards for its catch. A series of pictures combined with time. @ Thalangama Lake. **HdeS

This is a bird that can hover in stationary position. The spread-out tail is used to 'float' in one place, while the wings flap 8 times a second. The usual prey can spot the bird even at 15 meters. Once locked on to a prey very high up in the sky, it begins its controlled and coordinated descent. When the beak hits the water it suddenly slows down 200 times to reduce widespread ripples that would warn the prey. Ref Lovearth.com BBC.

Feeding ritual @ Thalangama. **HdeS

A mating sequence of the **White-throated Kingfisher**, a total of 39 pictures in 9 seconds! Only some are shown. While on the boat, Hotel Ranweli, Negombo, the guide notified of a Kingfisher feeding a young one. I realized that it was a ritual before mating and brought the boat closer to the bank. **HdeS

Nesting, **White-throated Kingfisher** -
@ Thalangama Lake. A granite wall has not
deterred them from using ancestral property.
**HdeS

Oriental Dwarf Kingfisher also known as the Black-backed Kingfisher or Three-toed Kingfisher, the smallest in Sri Lanka, We waited for hours in Kitulgala on a Sunday while answering calls from Hospitals about patients. LakKumar missed a critical shot of the male feeding the female just before the mating took place, when he had to answer a telephone call about a Dengue patient. I was busy photographing the Monarch at the time. **HdeS

A mating sequence, of the, **Oriental Dwarf Kingfisher**, a very rare occasion. @ Sisira's Rest Kitulgala. **LF

Straight out of an ODEL tee Shirt! **HdeS

Backdrop of the Elephant Rock @ Yala. **HdeS

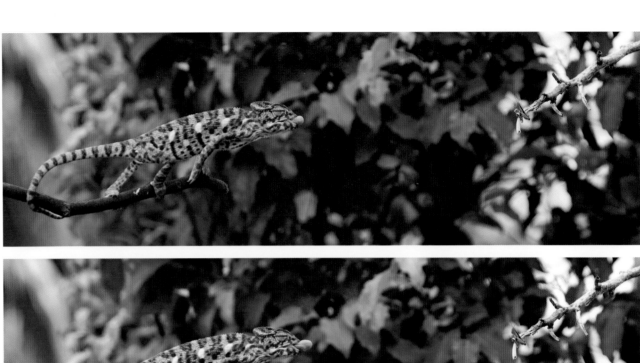

An interesting sequence of a **Chameleon** (known locally as Bodilima - Sinhala) catching a grasshopper. All 6 pictures were within one second. @ Domestic garden in Eluwankulama. **HdeS

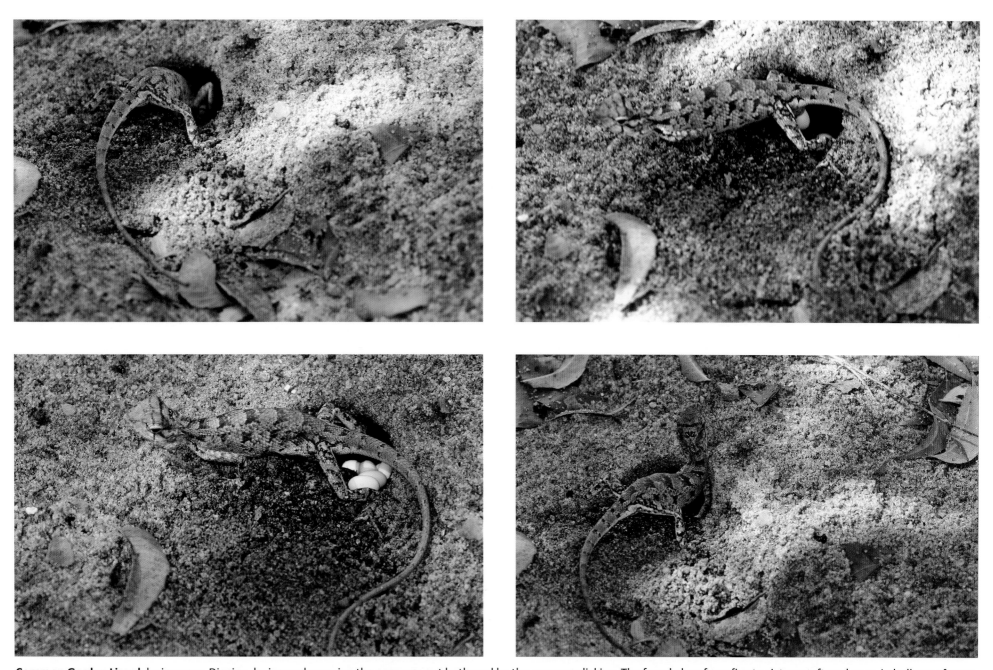

Common Garden Lizard, laying eggs. Digging, laying and covering the eggs was not bothered by the cameras clicking. The female lays from five to sixteen soft oval eggs, in hollows of trees, or in holes in the soil which they have burrowed, afterward covering them up. The young appear in about eight or nine weeks. @ Bundala Saltern bungalow. **HdeS

Common Garden Lizard, Male. The ground-colour is generally a light brownish olive, but the lizard can change it to bright red, to black, and to a mixture of both. This change is most often confined to the head, at other times diffused over the whole body and tail. **LF

A rapidly colour changing Common **Green Forest Lizard** and notice the sloughing of skin. A phenomenon often referred to by the common man as a political phenomenon! Sinhala Proverb: 'katussa wage pata maru karrane epa' (Don't change colours like a lizard). @ Kirinda, Neem Tree Resort. **HdeS

Mugger Crocodile basking in the sun. @ Bundala. **HdeS

The large female **Wood Spider** would have the tiny male for dinner after mating or if the female is hungry and the male gives the wrong signal. @ Kitulgala. **HdeS

Malabar Pied Hornbill male tossing before swallowing fruit. **PA

Malabar Pied Hornbill mating ritual. @ Yala. **HdeS

Malabar Pied Hornbill female with a lizard for breakfast. @ Habarana Chaaya Village. **HdeS

Male **Yellow Bittern** - "I spy you". Plays 'hide and seek' amongst the reed thicket. You would be lucky to get a glimpse of it. An uncommon bird, being elusive, makes the rarity more exciting.@ Debaraweva **HdeS

Black Bittern @ Thalangama **LF

The bittern eyes are placed on the sides of the head, giving the bird mostly monocular vision. Unlike most other birds, the eyes are placed low on the sides. It has an advantage of letting it to look for food underneath. When the bittern is alarmed, it stretches its head and neck up, pointing its bill to the sky. This gives the bird a slim outline, merging it with the surrounding vegetation, like grasses and sedges. It is known as the "Bittern stance" and it can maintain the position for many hours. In this defensive stance, the position of the eyes allows it to have a clear vision of the sky above as well as in front and horizontally at an approaching predator even though its bill points skyward.

Chestnut-headed Bee-Eater, a resident bird. @ Bundala. **HdeS

White-bellied Drongo, feeding its chicks.

It was interesting to see a Red-vented Bulbul also feeding these chicks. It transpired that the Bulbul nest was attacked by crows the previous day and it's babies taken as prey. @ Faculty of Medicine Ragama. **HdeS

White-bellied Drongo, always makes the cup shaped nest in a fork of a branch. Genetically 'imprinted' trait. @ Faculty of Medicine Ragama. **HdeS

Black Drongo The species is famous for its aggressive behavior towards much larger birds, such as crows, and even raptors, never hesitating to 'dive-bomb' any birds of prey that invades its territory Calls of raptors are mimicked by drongos and this behaviour is thought to aid in stealing food by alarming other birds that the drongos associate with. Reference Wikipedia @ Mannar. **HdeS

Crested Treeswift female. @ Bundala. **HdeS

Black-hooded Oriole always builds a hammock style nest. The instinct to build a nest with a particular architecture is imprinted genetically. A parent carefully feeding the baby. @ Faculty of Medicine Ragama. **HdeS

As soon as a movement, sound or vibration of a parent is seen or felt (but not when the wind blows) the brood open it's beaks while straining their necks upwards begging for food. The inside of the mouth, is bright usually red and is an indication of the site to place the food. In some birds, when food is placed blood is diverted to the stomach and intestine, thereby making the gape paler, then the parent knows which nestling has been fed or not. Ref. Life of Bids David Attenborough.

A Perfect Family. @ Minneriya. **LF

BIRD MIGRATION

One of the most challenging riddles is to find out how birds accurately and with apparently relative ease find their way often several thousands of miles away without a map, compass or GPS navigation.

The primary incentive for migration is for food. Longer days of warmer climates provide longer time for breeding birds to feed their young. This helps daytime birds to produce larger number of eggs 'clutches'. The primary physiological cue for migration is the change in the day length. These changes are also related to hormonal changes in the birds. As the daytime gets less in autumn, the birds migrate to warmer regions where there is little variation in available food with the seasons. These advantages counterbalance the high stress, physical exertion, and other dangers of the migration process such as predation. Predation is often high during migration. Long distance migration as young birds forms attachment to possible breeding sites and to favorite wintering sites. Once the attachment is made they show high location- faithfulness and go to the same wintering site over the years unless there are environmental changes, such as what happened in Bundala for flamingos and the island off Ambalangoda where thousands of terns laid eggs but now go away because of the hustle and bustle of the new harbor and dynamiting of fish. Flying in flocks reduces the energy cost. Flying in a V-formation may conserve 12–20% of the energy they would need to fly alone and may be faster. Waders are strong fliers and fly long distances often from the arctic region. For some species of shore birds (waders), migration realization hinge on the availability of certain important food resources at stopovers along the route. This gives them a chance to "refuel" for the next leg. Long distance migrants may have more than 50% of fat in the body to use as energy.

Some large broad-winged birds rely on thermal columns of rising hot air to enable them to soar. These include many birds of prey, and storks. These birds migrate in the daytime. It is known that European cuckoos abandon their eggs in an unsuspecting 'foster' bird's nest and fly back to Europe without the young. However, the young after being chased away when discovered, follow the same direction unvarying from generation to generation indicating an inborn or genetic imprinting and a drive in the brain to fly in a particular direction over a particular distance. Some birds that fly in the night very accurately use the star pattern although on cloudy nights they may get scattered or completely lost! Others that fly during the day use the position of the sun which may be more difficult because of the rapid movement of the sun. Most birds also have an internal clock to adjust for any errors.

There are others who probably use the North South magnetic fields to know the direction of flight. Microscopic iron oxide and magnetite elements have been found in the head of some birds. Fixing magnets to birds have shown to confuse them to find direction in experiments. Recent research shows a neural connection between the eye and "Cluster N", a part of the forebrain that is active during 'migrational orientation', suggesting that birds may actually be able to see the magnetic field of the earth.

Some birds also use huge landmarks such as canyons, lakes, mountains to guide them. At the destination they probably use their knowledge from previous years. Migratory routes and wintering regions are traditional and learned by young in their first migration with their older birds. Some ducks, such as the Garganey, move completely or partially into the tropics.

Basically they depend on the older bird's experience to guide the flock, while they may use multiple methods in the complex migration process where humans would definitely fail without complex navigation equipment!

It is unfortunate when humans are ignorant of bird's skills and therefore disregard a bird's life by destroying the environment or go bird hunting!

References
http://en.wikipedia.org/wiki /Bird_migration.
Winged Migration (2001) Documentary 98 mins.
http://www.imdb.com/title/tt0301727/

Chillaw Sandspit is a good place to spot birds. This **Wimbrel** was flying from one end to the other. It was difficult to photograph since it flew away with the slightest movement in the background and the Sandspits did not offer any camouflage. **HdeS

Crab Plover, an uncommon Wader was far away in the Mannar lagoon. I had to climb down from the road with my huge 300 MM 2.8 lens and fell down in the process. But it was worth it. **HdeS

Kentish Plover, male, a common breeding resident as well as migrant. @ Puttalam saltern. **HdeS

Wood Sandpiper @ Thalangama **LF

Greater Thick-knee @ Bundala **HdeS

Chillaw Sandspit – **Sanderlings** on the reef with the foamy waves in the background and the flock's synchronous movements is an interesting sight. It is a small wader, and a circumpolar Arctic (The region north of this circle is known as the Arctic, and the zone just to the south is called the Northern Temperate Zone) breeder, and is a long-distance migrant. **HdeS

Wood Sandpiper @ Bundala **HdeS

Little Ringed Plover @ Mundal **HdeS

Common Redshank @ Bundala **HdeS

Small Pratincole @ Bundala **HdeS

Rose-ringed Parakeet: Mating Ritual. One needs to ward off competitors! **HdeS

1, Necking! "You are beautiful". "He! He! You are tickling me!" Peeping tom: "Hey, Hey, what you doing with my girl!!"
2. "She is my gal now, you leave us alone!"
3. . "Let's get on with it, now that he is gone" "Mmmm... you are delicious!"
4. "I gave a Karate chop like this.... and that....., and he was down in no time!" "Rrealllly!"
5. "Oooh" "Aaah"

The kissing or billing may be a form of affection or regurgitation of food for each other

Alexandrine Parakeet. We were trying to photograph it on a tall tree when the flock got disturbed and started flying. It was a Crested Serpent Eagle that startled them. @ Uda Walawe. **HdeS

The **Sri Lanka Hanging Parrot**. Endemic bird finishing the Rambutans! Sisira's Rest Kitulgala. **HdeS

Tickell's Blue Flycatcher @ Kithulgala**HdeS

Turbulent moments, a **Western Reef Egret**, White Morph Chillaw. Note the distinctly heavy bill unusually black also the yellow legs up to the hock joint. **HdeS

Western Reef Egret Grey Morph, mostly dark slaty-grey plumage and a white throat. **PA

Little Egret: This Egret shows yellow up to hock joints typical of a Western Reef Egret but the bill is most important in separating the two forms. @ Chillaw Sandspits **HdeS

Intermediate Egret. @ Uda Walawe, struggling with a catch too big for him. But ultimately managed to satisfy its appetite. **LF

Great Egret with a prized catch any angler would be proud of! Unfortunately it lost the struggling potential victim when it tried to fly to another place. @ Bundala. **HdeS

We are in Love! Courting, **Great Egrets** in breeding Plumage. Note the red legs and the Greenish blue patch in between the eyes and the beak and the spreading fan of "bridal plumes" @ Ibbagamuwa wayside. **HdeS

Feeding two young hungry siblings is not an easy task. **Cattle Egrets** @Belum-mahara.**Hde S

Purple Heron, but has little or no purple although the background is. Usually adopts a 'catatonic' stance for long periods expecting a fish to arrive. @ Anevilindawa. **HdeS

Purple Heron. @ Thalangama Tank **LF

Purple Heron, juvenile. @ Thalangama Tank **HdeS

Lesser Adjutant – uncommon, has an ugly old bald man look. @ Kawudulla. **HdeS

The eerie look with an eel wrapped around the bill, straight off a Stephen Spielberg horror movie **HdeS

Grey Heron Catching the first light. @ Udawalawe **HdeS

Black-necked Stork @ Kumana. Very rare; seen in specific places Yala, Kumana, East and sometimes in the North. Since recently the Yala couple has not been seen **HdeS

A few **Spot-billed Pelicans** in the midst of a large flock of **Painted Storks** a beautiful sight. @ Yala **HdeS

A fantastic morning: **Spot-billed Pelicans** at conference with a **Painted Stork** as interpreter @ Bundala **HdeS

Spot-billed Pelicans although globally threatened are abundant in Sri Lanka and have spread throughout the country **HdeS

I was trying to take a picture of this Solitary **Pelican** when it suddenly lunged forward. The next few out of more than a dozen pictures in a few seconds tell the story of the unlucky victim the pouch @ Thalangama **HdeS

A beetle, confidently and defiantly walking into the Jaws of death of the **Black-headed Ibis**. @ Anevilundawa. **HdeS

Grey Francolin, in the backdrop of the early morning rising sun backlit cobwebs, dew and grass @ Puttalam. **HdeS

Tissa lake, tree reflections. 2006 **SdeS

Beruwela, Sunset 2009 **SdeS

Common Mime. @ Faculty of Medicine Ragama. **HdeS

Palm Fly. @ Faculty of Medicine Ragama **HdeS

The Tawny Coster @ Faculty of Medicine Ragama **HdeS

Tailed Jay, robust and restless fliers, very active butterflies and flutter their wings constantly, even when at flowers, hence difficult to photograph @ Faculty of Medicine Ragama **HdeS

Common Jezebel. @ Faculty of Medicine Ragama **HdeS

Common Birdwing. Largest in Sri Lanka. @ Faculty of Medicine Ragama. **HdeS

Grey Pansy. @ Faculty of Medicine Ragama **HdeS

Common Tiger @ Kolonnawa **HdeS

Pale palm Dart (*Telicota colon*). I was running around near the Medical Faculty sports ground With the camera when I noticed this butterfly which Looked more like a moth, a butterfly belonging to the family Hesperiidae. Only when I had a look at it on the computer did I realized that there was what immediately looked like a polythene clip on the head. Only later did I realize it was a Crab spider. @ Fac Med Ragama.
**HdeS

None of the different species of crab spiders build webs to trap insects including butterflies. Some are wandering hunters and the generally known are 'ambush predators'. Some species sit on or beside flowers, where they grab insects attracted to the flower. Some species look out for insects among leaves or bark, where they await the victim.

Pantala flavescens female **HdeS

Rhyothemis veriegata **HdeS

Diplocodes trivialis female **HdeS

Jewel Bug, (Metallic Shield Bug). (Scutelleridae). @ Mundel **HdeS

White-browed Bulbul. @ Faculty of Medicine Ragama, on a Dracaena tree. A careless and insensitive Gardener destroyed the nest while cutting grass. **HdeS

Indian Roller. The first time I saw a Roller at a distance I thought it was a Kingfisher because of the vibrant and exotic blue. The Sinhala name "Dumbonna" (Smoke Drinker), is because of its attraction to fires and smoke. This 'passive smoker' is addicted not to the smoke but the insects disturbed or attracted to the light of the fire. **LF

Banded Bay Cuckoo @ Kitulgala **HdeS

Jacobin Cuckoo, brood parasitism of Yellow- billed Babbler nests is known. @ Yala **HdeS

There was a huge gathering of jeeps on Padi khema in Yala, an usual site for **leopard** sightings. There were 4-5 leopards roaming around and snarling at an apparent rock! It took a while to realize it was a **crocodile** that had probably stolen the cats' previous day's prey while they were sleeping on trees. They dare not attack and were helpless onlookers till the croc jumped into the pool with the half eaten deer. **HdeS

Sri Lankan Leopard. The gracious, grandiose look in spite of defeat. **HdeS

Indian Muntjacs, also known as Barking Deer, is the mammal with the lowest recorded chromosome number, the male has a diploid number of 7, the female only 6 chromosomes.
@ Wilpattu **LF

117

Arugambay, Sunrise 2010. **SdeS

Hatton, dusk 2009 **SdeS

Brown-headed Barbet feeding the offspring. **HdeS

Brown-headed Barbet is known as a 'Jambu Kottorua' by some probably because of its attraction to the fruit. ** HdeS

Brown-headed Barbet, is also known in Sinhala as 'polos' (young Jack fruit) kottoruwa. It is feeding the chick with ripe Jack fruit (waraka). What is important is to note the scar on the side of the head caused in the process of defending the chick when a Shikra attacked the nest. ** HdeS

Brown-headed Barbet, removal of fecal material helps to improve nest sanitation, which in turn helps to increase the likelihood that nestlings will remain healthy. It also helps to reduce the chance that predators will see it or smell it and thereby find the nest. The waste matter is usually disposed away from the nest so that predators will not be able to locate the nest. Fecal sac is a mucous membrane, which surrounds the feces of some species of birds. Not all species generate fecal sacs. **HdeS

Crimson-fronted Barbet, young. @ Faculty of Medicine Ragama. **HdeS

Crimson-fronted Barbet, works like a carpenter chiseling away tree holes. Often makes many mock tree holes before nesting most probably to mislead predators. Faculty of Medicine Ragama. **HdeS

Yellow-fronted Barbet, endemic. We had finished photographing birds at Sisira's Rest and were driving back when we saw this one. @ Kitulgala. **LF

Inset, my very first bird photograph with a Sony digital that used 3.5 inch floppy disks! @ Trincomalee. **HdeS

Coppersmith Barbet. @ Uda Walawe. **HdeS

Brown Hawk Owl Opposite Royal College **HdeS

Juvenile. @ Rehab Hosp Ragama **LF

Vision of nocturnal birds: Based on the size of their eyes alone, one might guess that owls see extremely well. Their eyes are much larger in proportion to the sizes of their heads than our eyes are in order to improve their efficiency, especially under low light conditions. In fact, the eyes are so well developed, that they are not eye balls as such, but elongated tubes. They are held in place by bony structures in the skull called Sclerotic rings. For this reason, an owl cannot "roll" or move its eyes, that is, it can only look straight ahead. Owls more than makes up for this by being able to turn its head up to 270 degrees left or right from the forward facing position, and almost upside down. The forwards facing eyes limits the field of vision to 110^0 but the binocular (three dimensional) view is really wide (70^0). At the same time the retina is packed with rods rather than cones for Black and White for the night. In addition the pupils and cornea are relatively huge to allow more light. Owls can see in light up-to 100 times less, than what a human eye could discern

This **Barn Owl** of 'Legend of the Guardians: The Owls of Ga'Hoole' fame, was by the roadside off Initum Rd, Dehiwala. News of this sighting spread like wildfire . Unfortunately folklore like in Ga'Hoole' set in, 'that it brings bad luck' and some households in the area managed to chase the bird away. The ears of owls are also placed asymmetrically increasing the time lag between the arrival at each ear of the same sound wave with 2 points of coordinates, so as to allow the bird to pinpoint the source of the sound. Barn Owls, can also track their prey only by sound, without any visual clues. In an experiment they put an owl and a mouse in a darkened cage without any light, and the owl was able to pounce precisely on it's prey. The flat face of some owls also act like a 'satellite dish' with a rim of stiff feathers which collects and channels sounds inwards towards the ears on either side of the eyes. In addition the 'dish' may be divided in the middle with a line of bristles that would enhance 'stereo' type of sound and then the eyes focus on the prey to fix its gaze. The ears and eyes coordinate to direct the bird to the accurate position followed by the talons that hit the target in the coordination loop in the neural circuit with pinpoint precision. Ref. Lovearth. com, BBC Worldwide. **HdeS

Collared Scops Owl. @ Ragama Medical Faculty. Ear tufts in owls, have nothing to do with hearing. @ Faculty of Medicine Ragama. **HdeS

Brown Fish Owl @ Uda Walave **LF

Chestnut-backed Owlet, This species is diurnal. It can often be located by the small birds that mob it while it is perched in a tree. It feeds mainly on insects, such as beetles, but also captures mice, small lizards, and small birds mostly when the young are being fed. Endemic. @ Kitulgala. **HdeS

The hungry young owlets waiting for the parents to bring breakfast, The innocent transform In to a monster like in a Spielberg movie!

VISION OF DIURNAL BIRDS OF PREY

A kestrel hovering five hundred feet above can swoop down and in the final pounce take a grasshopper from the top of a stem of grass. It had seen the grasshopper clearly from a high position in the sky. Sharpness of eyesight is difficult to describe but if we had the vision of a kestrel it is likely that we could read a newspaper at 25 yards. A Kestrel has a visual field of 150^0 and binocular field of 50^0. With the sight of an eagle we should be able to identify the jerk of a rabbit from a distance of two miles. There has to be physiological explanations to explain all this. Firstly, the eyes of birds of prey are comparably larger than the eyes of other vertebrates, enabling larger and sharper visual images. If the eyes of humans were to be alike, the eyes would be the size of cricket balls.

The retina is about two times as thick as the human retina and has consistently more sensory cells in the upper half of the retina which helps a bird observe images when looking down from a perch or whilst flying. It is surprising in having two very sensitive spots on the retina or "foveae" compared with only one fovea in the human. The necessity for two foveae is obvious when we consider that most birds use their eyes in two different ways: monocularly, with eyes facing sideways and binocularly (three dimensionally), with eyes facing forwards. There should be a sensitive area on the retina opposite the optic axis of the lens when the eye is looking sideways and this, since it lies near the central part of the retina, is known as the central fovea. When the eye is turned to look forwards as in binocular vision, the main axis of the optic system of the eye moves across the retina to its outer boundary and there is a second sensitive area, known as the temporal fovea. These two sensitive areas are separately termed the "search" fovea and the "pursuit" fovea, since the first is employed in the sideways vision used when searching for prey and food, whilst the second is used in forward binocular vision after the prey has been located, 'position locked', and the pursuit is on.

The retina consists normally of a large number of tiny light-sensitive cells, known from their shapes as cones, and rods. The cones arc the cells whereby we distinguish colours, but they are operative only at relatively high light intensities. At very low light-intensities, only the rods can record. In the kestrel the number reaches the astonishing figure of around 1,000,000 visual cells per square millimeter in the foveal region. The visual acuity of the kestrel's eye is approximately eight times that of the human eye.

Presume two intense points of light, very close to each other, are viewed from far. If these as two points of light are to be visualized, it is necessary that the images of the two points should fall on separate and discrete cells in the retina. If it falls together on a single cell, it cannot be recorded as separate. Therefore for very fine resolution, the eye needs a retina with a large number of cones each distinct by itself, capable of sending back to the brain separate, different impression. In other words the retina is like a CMOS sensor in a digital camera with very high resolution that could pick on tiny parts and colours of a bird's feather far away.

In 1995 a discovery was made by Finnish scientists that some birds of prey see a wider colour spectrum than we do, including ultraviolet light. Kestrels are a familiar sight hovering along grassland. They watch out for small rodents. Their prey is fast and agile and ranges over surroundings that are often homogeneous and widespread. However, rodents mark their 'runs' (territories) as with dogs with urine and faeces, which are visible in ultraviolet light. Wild kestrels are able to detect vole and mouse latrine scents in ultraviolet settings. This enables them to screen large areas of grassland in relatively quick time.

Common Kestrel, this picture was taken along with a British Paediatrician and birder Gregory (who came to examine at the MD exam) to @ Walawe.

Amur Falcon (vagrant). It was a long and tiring day we were returning from Yala and about to turn in to our guest house in Kirinda (Temple Flower) when our driver Sampath shouted "anna (there) Kestral, kestrel". It was dark and I was reluctant to pull out the camera just for a Kestrel on a wire in low light! However, in spite of the strong winds the bird was clinging on to the wire. With great reluctance I started shooting and the bird was continuing to pose. It was too difficult to really identify the bird, when I looked at it on the lap top, it was weird with orange legs! I emailed it to Lester who immediately identified it and phoned me with great excitement. @ Kirinda. **HdeS

The Amur Falcon has one of the extensive raptor movements. It is also unique because it supposedly flies a long distance over the sea and it has different routes to and from its breeding grounds and it supposedly flies several thousands of miles on its journey across the sea. Recent satellite data has shown that they fly a distance 2,500 to 3,100km over the sea in spring and do this by flying non-stop for between 2 and 3 days. They have stop over points on their migration route back to the breeding grounds, and fly south of the Himalayas in northern India. They are also capable of covering huge amounts of distance in a few days and were able to travel up much of Africa in only a few days. Satellite tracking of raptors on migration is a crucial tool in studying the courses taken by birds. It is very useful when used where there are small chance of recovering ringed birds. Previously, it was not possible to track any of the small falcons due to the size of the satellite transmitters. However, new transmitters are small not to affect the survival of the birds. The Amur Falcon travels over a very long distance (Eastern China to southern Africa). In October 2012, Conservation India documented the shocking massacre of tens of thousands of migrating Amur falcons (*Falco amurensis*) in the remote state of Nagaland in north-eastern India. Shashank Dalvi and Ramki Sreenivasan estimate that between 120,000 and 140,000 Amur falcons are being slaughtered every year in NE India.

http://www.africanraptors.org/amur-falcon-migration-route-finallyplotted/

Juvenile, **White-bellied Sea Eagle**. Bundala.** HdeS

Small as it may be, but a **White-browed Fantail** mobbing a **Changeable Hawk Eagle**, Uda Walawe. There was a nesting of the smaller bird nearby. A mocking bird might fly in front of a predator to divert it away from the brood. **HdeS

A Majestic Looking, Juvenile, **Changeable Hawk Eagle**. The Prince has already taken the powers of the King as often happens! @ Kawudulla. **HdeS

An adult **Changeable Hawk Eagle**, They always are majestic. @ Yala**HdeS

Changeable Hawk Eagle. I waited for a long time to get this moment. One disadvantage of many people going in the crowd is, some of the uninterested persons who come to see a deer, an Elephant or a crocodile start moaning often making you impatient and also disturbing the birds. @ Uda Walawe. **HdeS

Shaheen is the local resident race of the **Peregrine Falcon** in Sri Lanka. It is the fastest bird and is adapted to taking prey of medium sized birds such as pigeons and parrots in the air and can achieve a speed of 240 kmh in level flight; when diving after prey it can exceed speeds of 320 kmh. It tucks in the wings to become a tear drop shaped 'missile' giving aerodynamic advantage. The upper beak is notched near the tip, which enables it to kill prey by severing the spinal column at the neck. An estimate of 40 breeding pairs in Sri Lanka was made in 1996. The dive could damage a bird's lungs, but small bony tubercles on a falcon's nostrils guide the powerful airflow away from the nostrils, while diving by reducing the change in air pressure. To protect their eyes, the falcons use their nictitating membranes (third eyelids) to spread tears and clear debris from their eyes while maintaining vision during the dive. (http://www.extremescience.com/peregrine-falcon-video.htm). @ Polonnanruwa. **LF

Shikra, female, In Sinhala it is referred to as Kurulu Goya (Bird stalker), squirrels, small birds, small reptiles, lizards and insects are it's prey. Small birds may dive through foliage to avoid a Shikra, and Small Kingfishers have been observed diving into water. Babblers (yellow-billed – 'seven sisters') may rally together to mob and drive away a Shikra. @ Polonnaruwa. **LF

06:47:10 AM   06:47:17 AM   06:47:19 AM   06:47:20 AM

4 photographs combined to show the sequence of a **Brahminy Kite**, feeding on a fish in Mid-Air a ten second sequence. @ Chillaw Sandspits. **HdeS

A Juvenile, **Brahminy Kite**. @ Bundala. **HdeS

Black-winged Kite. It is known to hover over open grasslands in the manner of the much smaller kestrels. @ Polonnaruwa **LF

An attack, on a **Black kite**, by **Crows** competing for food. @ Mannar. **HdeS

Mobbing behavior includes flying above the intruder, dive bombing, loud squawking and excreting on the predator. Mobbing can also be used to drive larger birds away from food. One bird might distract while others swiftly take the food.

A great show of unity by the powerless against the mighty! While trying to photograph **Gulls** on the beach of Mannar, we saw a huge commotion. In a distance I saw a lone raptor trying to dive into the sea but repeatedly prevented by a handful of crows and Gulls. The sun was up and the light was extreme; however I started aiming at the faraway birds and started taking pictures with the maximum speed to catch all the action. Out of a large number of pictures taken only 7 are reproduced. In short, a Juvenile **White-bellied Sea Eagle** had struck a **Heuglin's Gull** that was helplessly struggling and horrified in the water. The eager Eagle had only very little more to do to grab the prey and fly off! However, the might of unity was shown when the small birds gathered in numbers very fast including many Crows to chase the Eagle away! (pic 7) The power of unity to chase away injustice irrespective of the species is clearly shown here. If this happened in the human arena, there would have been mainly onlookers the 'passive perpetrators' of injustice!

Mobbing is an anti-predator behavior, when a certain species mob a predator by supportively attacking or pestering it. It is usually to protect their offspring who are frequently preyed upon. The interesting aspect here was to see the crows joining the gulls , suppose the eagle was the common enemy. Birds that breed in colonies such as gulls are widely seen to attack intruders. **HdeS

Unsuccessful attempt at catching the Gull, chased away by the mob the juvenile **White-bellied Sea Eagle** then flew over us. **HdeS

The **Crested Serpent Eagle**, one dare not ruffle it's feathers! It is a specialist reptile eater. Spends most of the day perched and usually looking for food. They appear to use a sit and wait strategy for ages. @ Wilpattu **LF

Black Headed Munia @ Uda Walawe **HdeS

White Rumped Munia Front Garden **HdeS

Scaly-breasted Munias specialise in eating grass seeds and sedges, and have large conical beaks adapted for this purpose. **LF

Sri Lanka Blue Magpie, an endemic, is the 'Playboy icon' for the cover page of most Sri Lankan bird books! Probably one of the most colorful and attractive birds, although the behavior is often not in keeping to it's looks; but that of a crow, the family it belongs to. **HdeS

The large number of **Greater Flamingos**, that were there in Bundala are hardly seen now. An occasional flock of a few birds still come for short periods. Over ambitious irrigation projects that may alter the salinity in the water probably had an effect of the micro flora of the water that is the food for the flamingo. **HdeS

Unlike many other species of chicks that fend for itself, adults feed their chicks a secretion of the upper digestive tract referred to as 'crop milk', somewhat similar to milk produced by pigeons. 'Milk' secretion is caused by the hormone prolactin produced also by mammals, which both the male and female flamingo produce. Milk is 8% to 9% protein and 15% fat. It has also been shown to contain anti-oxidants and immune-enhancing factors, red and white cells similar to mammal milk but is red due to the pigment canthaxanthin. These chicks stock this pigment in the liver, to be used when adult feathers grow. Parents are able to recognize their own chick by sight and vocalizations. They will feed no other chick. Parents also keep a close, protective watch on their chick as it explores its habitat. Chicks gather in large groups called crèches.

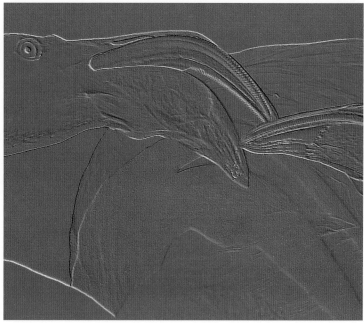

Blue-green and red algae, diatoms, larval and adult forms of small insects, molluscs and crustaceans make up the main food of **flamingos**. A flamingo's pink or reddish feather and other colouration come from a diet high in alpha and beta carotenoids. Standing in shallow water it allows the bills to hang upside-down facing backward in the water and sweeping their heads from side to side. Flamingo filters its food with a spiny, piston-like tongue that aids in sucking food-filled water past the lamellae inside the curved bill.

A modified close up Picture of a Flamingo from the zoo shows the filtering plate grooves clearly. **HdeS

Lesser Goldenback (Black-rumped Flameback), we observed from the time of excavating the nest hole until the eggs hatched. The same level for photography was achieved from the Pharmacology Department upstairs. @ Ragama Medical Faculty. **HdeS

Yellow-crowned Woodpecker. Rare bird. Was taken with my old Canon EOS 350, @ Bundala **HdeS

06:53:25 AM   06:53:24 AM   06:53:24 AM   06:53:24 AM   06:53:23 AM   06:53:23 AM

Series of Photographs with timing, in 2 seconds the tern is off with an insignificant fish. I sat on the ground in an island in the Puttalam saltern with LakKumar and watched the **Whiskered Terns** fishing for more than an hour. It was only after several attempts to get a good sequence that I was successful. **HdeS

Lesser Crested Tern. Chillaw Sandspits **HdeS

Heuglin's Gull, 1st winter @ Mannar ** HdeS

Brown-headed Gull @ Mannar ** HdeS

Common Tern, the bird was stealing from a fishing net brought ashore. @ Kalpitiya ** HdeS

Common Tern. @Kalpitiya **HdeS

Little Tern. The simplest nest construction is the scrape, which is merely a shallow depression in soil or vegetation. It is deep enough to keep the eggs from rolling away, is lined with bits of sea shell fragments. It also helps to prevent them from sinking into muddy or sandy soil if the nest is accidentally flooded. Eggs and young in scrape nests are more exposed @ Mannar **LF

Ashy Woodswallow. The bird flew in swift style and initially confused the identification. At first we could not find who the parent was and who was being fed! It is obvious here who the baby is although there is no difference in size! A wasp being fed. In some birds the young may be fed to size even heavier than the adult, and this would ensure food stores that may be needed when the young bird has to fend for itself and finding adequate food may be a problem at the beginning for rapid growth of nestling, frequent small feeding is necessary and higher content of protein is needed. Therefore in some species the young may be fed as much as 70% as animal protein as compared to the adult who may take only 5% of animal proteins. @ Anewilundawa. **LF

Serenity of a sunset on the coast 2011. **SdeS

A calm rural setting 2010. **SdeS

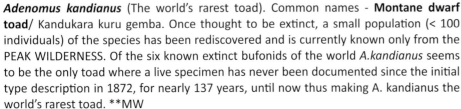

Adenomus kandianus (The world's rarest toad). Common names - **Montane dwarf toad**/ Kandukara kuru gemba. Once thought to be extinct, a small population (< 100 individuals) of the species has been rediscovered and is currently known only from the PEAK WILDERNESS. Of the six known extinct bufonids of the world *A.kandianus* seems to be the only toad where a live specimen has never been documented since the initial type description in 1872, for nearly 137 years, until now thus making A. kandianus the world's rarest toad. **MW

Pseudophilautus stellatus (Kelaart 1853) has been rediscovered from the Peak Wilderness, Central Hills of Sri Lanka. The species known only from its now lost holotype, was the first shrub frog described from Sri Lanka (Ceylon), and had not been reported since then. It was thought to have become extinct for nearly 157 years. Prior to the rediscovery *P. stellatus* has been witnessed only by two people. It is the only known extinct amphibian without any type material, photographs or drawings, for the longest period of time thus making it the world's rarest amphibian. (This finding is to be published in the Journal of Zootaxa: Lost and found: The world's most elusive amphibian, Pseudophilautus stellatus (Kelaart 1853) rediscovered. (L. J. Mendis Wickramasinghe, Dulan Ranga Vidanapathirana, Sameera Ariyarathne, Gehan Rajeev, Amila Chanaka, Jennifer Pastorini, Gayan Chathuranga and Nethu Wickramasinghe)

Pseudophilautus hoffmanni (Endangered Species). Common names- **Hoffman's shrub frog**/ Hoffmange panduru madiya. A species restricted to the Knuckels massif, populated in an area less than 500 km2, and found nowhere else in the world. With ever increasing land encroachments for various cultivations, and harmful activities by us. Their populations are now highly threatened. **MW

Pseudophilautus mooreorum (Endangered Species) Common names **Moore's shrub frog**/ Moorege panduru madiya. This copulating duo were captured from the Knuckels massif, and is found only in this region, in an area less than 500km2 and found nowhere else in the world. Its breeding behavior is still not known. This sighting is one of the first observations of the species in amplexus in the wild. **MW

Pseudophilautus schmarda (Endangered Species) Common names- **Schmarda's shrub frog**/ Gorahandi panduru madiya. **MW

Pseudophilautus femoralis (Endangered Species). Common names- **Leaf nesting shrub frog**/ Pala panduru madiya. Endemic to the central highlands, found in 1200 m above sea level. This frog can only be observed in an area of less than 500 km2 from the whole planet. Easily identified from its luminous green colouration, this beautiful frog is found in Nuwara-eliya, Horton plains, Haggala, and Sri Pada. **MW

Coeloganthus helena. Common names- **Trinket snake/** Kata kaluwa. This is a harmless snake. Its Sinhala name rightly suggests 'katakaluwa', since inside of its mouth is black in colour. Due to myths and misconceptions in the country these reptiles are feared for and killed. **MW

Boiga barnesii (Near threatened). Common names- **Barne's cat snake/**Panduru mapila. This rare harmless snake is the only endemic cat snake in Sri Lanka. Cat snakes all over the world are arboreal (tree dwelling) and are active nocturnally. Restricted to the wet-zone forest and surrounding habitats, it has been categorized as Near Threatened according to the 2007 IUCN Red List. **MW

Boiga ceylonensis Common names- **Sri Lankan cat snake**/ Nidi mapila. **MW

Albino Cobra **MW

Prionailurus viverrinus Common names- **Fishing cat**/ Handun diviya. A kitten playing under the morning rays. They dwell in habitats close to water bodies, and are nocturnal. Their populations are threatened with habitat loss and decreasing quality of water in water bodies. **MW

Loris lydekkerianus (Near threatened). Common names- **Gray Slender Loris**/ Alu unahapuluwa. These nocturnal primates are found in the dry zone parts of the island. Its numbers are fast declining due to rapid decrease in forest covers, of the dry zone. **MW

Loris tardigradus (Endangered Species) Common names- **Sri Lanka Red Slender Loris**/ Sri Lanka Rath Unahapuluwa. A quite small nocturnal primate, found in the lowland southern wet zone forests, and is highly threatened by ever increasing human population which has led to its habitat loss and degradation. **MW

Serendib Scops Owl endemic @ Kitulagala **UH

Sri Lanka Bay Owl @ Kitulagala **UH

Sri Lankan Frogmouth. They are nocturnal and are found in wooded areas. The plumage bear a resemblance to that of dried leaves and as they perch on branches, sitting still and resembling a dry branch, making it particularly challenging to find. It has a wide and hooked bill with slit nostrils and the large head has the eyes facing frontward to provide a wide field of binocular vision. **UH

Yellow Eared Bulbul, Endemic **UH

Black Capped Bulbul, Endemic **UH

Sri Lanka Wood Pigeon, Endemic. @ Sinharaja **UH

Scaly Thrush, Endemic @ Sinharaja **UH

Rufous Horseshoe Bat **UH

False Vampire bat **UH

Fruit bat @ Town Hall Colombo **HdeS

Sri Lankan White eye. Endemic. This bird appears in a 35 cents Sri Lankan postal stamp first issued in 1983**UH

Sri Lankan Spurfowl. a member of the pheasant family which is endemic to the dense rainforests of Sri Lanka. It is a very secretive bird, and despite its size is difficult to see as it slips through dense undergrowth. Appears in a one rupee Sri Lankan postal stamp**UH

Sri Lanka Wood-shrike, endemic **UH

Layard's Parakeet, endemic is a bird of forests, particularly at the edges and in clearings. Appears on a 50 cents Sri Lankan postal stamp. **UH

Spot-winged Thrush, endemic @ Kithulgala**LF

Scaly Thrush, endemic @ Singharaja **LF

Sinharaja 2012 **SdeS

Haputhale 2010 **SdeS

Sri Lankan Leopard enjoying a Siesta after chasing deer. Let's not wake up sleeping Leopards. Kotigala (Wepandeniya) @ Yala **PA

Sri Lankan Leopard and cub Meda para @ Yala **PA

Childhood is so wonderful playing "join the train". Hopefully not training for the zoo show!! @ Minneriya **PA

Nursery playtime 'Mega leap-frog' @ Minneriya **PA

Sri Lankan Leopard in a relaxed mood . Can afford to relax since there are hardly any predators for them (other than humans) **PA

Leopard, A Vantage point for surveillance **PA

The Sri Lankan Sloth Bear the only bear species found in Sri Lanka, and the sub species is endemic to the island. Feeds on nuts, berries, and roots, one of its main staples is insects, which it removes from rotting stumps and trees with its long, hairless snout. It rarely kills animals but would occasionally feed on carrion as well. Note the distinct three pairs of mammary glands. It is highly threatened, with a wild population of less than 500 in the many isolated groups with a decrease in numbers. Destruction of dry-zone natural forest for 'development' is its main threat, since it is highly dependent on natural forests for its food source.

This mother had 3 cubs @ Yala **PA, a rare occurrence.

A Family Portrait @ Kalaweva **PA

European Bee-eater. It is strongly migratory, wintering in tropical Africa, India and Sri Lanka. An extremely rare migrant on the electric fence for elephants @Lunugamwehera National Park. After taking off for an insect, It always came back and settled there **PA

Sri Lanka Scimitar Babbler. It is endemic to the island. @ Kitulgala **PA

Red-faced Malkoha is a member of the cuckoo order of birds. It is endemic to Sri Lanka although some old records have apparently erroneously referred to its presence in southern India. @ The biodiversity 'Hotspot' in Sri Lanka Sinharaja forest. It is classified as 'vulnerable' **PA

"Let's start a family" **IR

Chital or spotted deer **IR

Leopard, 'better not follow it' **IR

Tusker @ Kalaweva **IR

Sambar **IR

Wild Buffalo. The IUCN considers the wild forms of Water Buffalo under Bubalus arnee, while the domestic forms are considered under B. bubalis **IR

Leopard big yawn after a nocturnal hunt **IR

References

The Life of Birds by David Attenborough (Hardcover - September 28, 1998) Princeton University Press, Princeton, New Jersey ISBN: 9780691016337

Life of Birds (documentary) Presented by David Attenborough, Composers Ian Butcher, Steven Faux (English), 10 episodes. Executive producers Mike Salisbury. Produced by BBC Natural History Unit, PBS.

Birds of Sri Lanka. (Helm Field Guides) by Deepal Warakagoda, Carol Inskipp, Tim Inskipp and Richard Grimmett (Jun 1, 2012). Publisher: A&C Black; 1st edition (June 1, 2012) ISBN-10: 071368853X

A Photographic Guide to Birds of Sri Lanka. Gehan De Silva Wijeyeratne, Deepal Warakagoda, T. S. U. De Zylva. Publisher: Ralph Curtis Publishing (February 1, 2001) ISBN-10: 1859745113

A Guide to the Birds of Sri Lanka by the late G. M. Henry (Author), Edited by Thilo W. Hoffmann, Deepal Warakagoda, Upali Ekanayake. Oxford University Press, USA; 3 edition (August 27, 1998) ISBN-10: 0195638131

Book of British Birds (Readers Digest) Readers Digest; 3rd edition (March 27, 2003) ISBN-10: 0276427459

Wikipedia, the free encyclopedia. http://en.wikipedia.org/wiki/Main_Page

Prof Harendra de Silva MBBS, DCH MSc (Birm), FRCP (Lond & Edin), FRCPCH, FCGP, FSLCP, FCPS (Pak), FCCP, is the Senior Professor of Paediatrics at the faculty of Medicine Ragama. Having started his career as a consultant paediatrician at Karapitiya in 1983 he moved through many areas of his specialty doing both clinical work and valuable research. Having brought the country's attention to the importance of child protection he served as the founder Chairmen of Sri Lanka's National Child Protection Authority (NCPA) He is a person with wide interests that include areas like Bonsai, Energy conservation and solar power, gemology and hoteling. He was the recipient of many awards which include, Most Outstanding Asian Paediatrician(2003), Senior Ashoka Fellow for Social Entrepreneurship by the Ashoka Foundation (Wash DC), Distinguished Career award by the International Society against Child Abuse and Neglect (USA) 2006. He was among top 10 nominated by the prestigious British Medical Journal for life time achievements in 2010. harendra51@gmail.com

Dr LakKumar Fernando MBBS, DCH, MD, MRCP, MRCPCH FRCP (Lond), Is a Consultant Paediatrician of repute with over 14 years' of experience as a specialist. He is well known internationally as a dengue expert and took the initiative to change the dengue management guidelines in Sri Lanka. He is also a contributor to the recent WHO Guideline on the management of dengue(2011). He was invited to Pakistan for help in 2011 during their major dengue epidemic and his work in Pakistan received their highest level of appreciation. He is a devoted clinician and was adjudged the best consultant by the Ministry of Health Sri Lanka at the National Health Excellence awards 2007. Recently he was also awarded the Senior Ashoka Fellowship (Wash DC). Presently he is attached to General Hospital Negombo. lakkumar@gmail.com

Sandun de Silva started his journey into photography 7 years ago while he was working at LT times as the Associate Editor borrowing his father's camera. Around the same time he worked on Ford Supermodel Search Sri Lanka after which he took up professional photography permanently. He has been the official photographic partner for Colombo fashion week for the last 5 years and has since worked on many brands as a commercial fashion and advertising photographer. His spectrum in photography is wide and include architectural and wedding photography and extends to Maldives too. Being a leading fashion and model photographer in Sri Lanka he is involved as a trainer and lecturer in various forms of photographic workshops. He has also done CSR work for the Thalassemia fund raising, Light of Change, British Council and others. He is also a qualified Cordon Bleu chef. sands696@yahoo.co.uk, www.sandundesilva.com

L. J. Mendis Wickramasinghe is the founder and the President of the Herpetological Foundation of Sri Lanka. He has close to two decades of field herpetological (reptile and amphibian) experience in Sri Lanka with a focus on taxonomic identifications with close to 20 new species of reptiles and amphibians discovered so far, and also provides education and awareness to the general public on Venomous Snakes in the island. He has contributed his expertise towards national projects on identification of threatened species in Sri Lanka, and has facilitated the declaration of several protected areas in Sri Lanka. A member of the Expert Committee on herpetofauna in Sri Lanka, under the National Species Conservation Advisory Group (NSCAG), and is in several international bodies including several Species Survival Commission groups of the International Union for Conservation of Nature (IUCN/SSC). Scuba diving, survival techniques and tracking, bird watching and natural history are other areas of interest. boiga2000@gmail.com,

Palitha Antony developed an interest in photography and wildlife during school years and wildlife photography has been his passion for many years as a result; He is thus ideally situated to study and photograph the wide diversity of plant and animal life in the country. His work has been published in journals, magazines, calendars, books, and many newspaper articles locally and internationally. His photographs has won prizes and have been highly commended in photographic competitions locally and internationally. Palitha works as a manager in the pharmaceutical industry. explopalitha@gmail.com

Uditha Hettige is an internationally well-known professional birder, researcher and wildlife enthusiast, with over 24 years' experience in studying the wildlife of Sri Lanka. He leads tours in Sri Lanka and India. He is a leading wildlife sound recordist in Sri Lanka, and coauthor of "Bird sounds and images of birds of Sri Lanka" CD - ROM guide. He is also a wildlife artist. udithabirder@gmail.com , www.birdandwildlifeteam.com

Ifham Raji. Gem dealer, almost full time photographer and now an hotelier, he is a person who was taking wild life seriously from a young age. Switches between Canon and Nikon from time to time, funded by the gems and jewels! His pictures are real 'Gems". ifham@jmmraji. com>. wwww.jmmraji.com. www.ifhamrajiimages.com, www.raajmahsl.com

Lester Perera is an internationally acclaimed fanatical professional birder, researcher and wild life enthusiast, with over 25 years' experience in bird watching alone, and is undeniably one of the most accomplished bird artist in the region. He has held over half a dozen solo bird art exhibitions in Sri Lanka and exhibited his work at many international exhibitions. He has travelled extensively in India leading wildlife and bird watching guiding tours for over a decade and has a massive list of South Asian birds seen by him as a result. lesterceyx@yahoo.com, www.birdandwildlifeteam.com

Grey-headed Fish Eagle @ Bundala **HdeS